HIGH PRAISE FOR *FIRST WE QUIT OUR JOBS*

"**Wonderfully written,** charmingly intimate. The adventures of two escape artists from the big city rat race who set out to explore North America, each other and a life without pressure. A fantasy we all can share."

> —Nathaniel Branden, Ph.D.,
> psychologist and author of
> *The Art of Living Consciously*

"FIRST WE QUIT OUR JOBS **makes the fantasy a reality.** In an honest, unpretentious style, Marilyn Abraham loosens the knot of corporate competition and meetings of the bored and takes to the road. If you've ever thought about discovering freedom, rediscovering loved ones and starting over, begin here."

> —Warren Farrell, Ph.D., author of
> *The Myth of Male Power* and
> *Why Men Are the Way They Are*

"**It starts like a prison-escape movie** then turns into a pica-resque travelogue and winds up . . . well, it never really does end, which is the point of the book. Marilyn Abraham's excellent adventure begins anew on almost every page. What fun she's had!"

> —Jane and Michael Stern

"For anyone who's ever fantasized about chucking it all and hitting the open road in search of America and yourself, **this book is a must read.** Abraham is a graceful and zesty writer whose experience goes to the heart of the searching baby boomer at midlife."

> —Wanda Urbanska and Frank Levering,
> authors of *Moving to a Small Town*
> and *Simple Living*

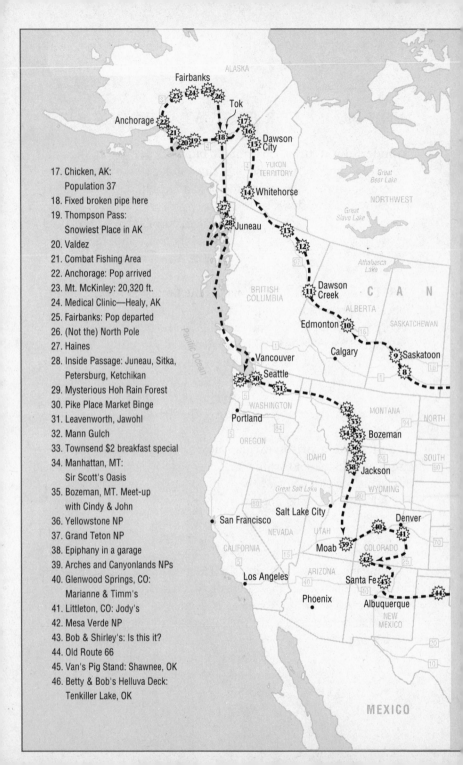

17. Chicken, AK:
    Population 37
18. Fixed broken pipe here
19. Thompson Pass:
    Snowiest Place in AK
20. Valdez
21. Combat Fishing Area
22. Anchorage: Pop arrived
23. Mt. McKinley: 20,320 ft.
24. Medical Clinic—Healy, AK
25. Fairbanks: Pop departed
26. (Not the) North Pole
27. Haines
28. Inside Passage: Juneau, Sitka,
    Petersburg, Ketchikan
29. Mysterious Hoh Rain Forest
30. Pike Place Market Binge
31. Leavenworth, Jawohl
32. Mann Gulch
33. Townsend $2 breakfast special
34. Manhattan, MT:
    Sir Scott's Oasis
35. Bozeman, MT. Meet-up
    with Cindy & John
36. Yellowstone NP
37. Grand Teton NP
38. Epiphany in a garage
39. Arches and Canyonlands NPs
40. Glenwood Springs, CO:
    Marianne & Timm's
41. Littleton, CO: Jody's
42. Mesa Verde NP
43. Bob & Shirley's: Is this it?
44. Old Route 66
45. Van's Pig Stand: Shawnee, OK
46. Betty & Bob's Helluva Deck:
    Tenkiller Lake, OK

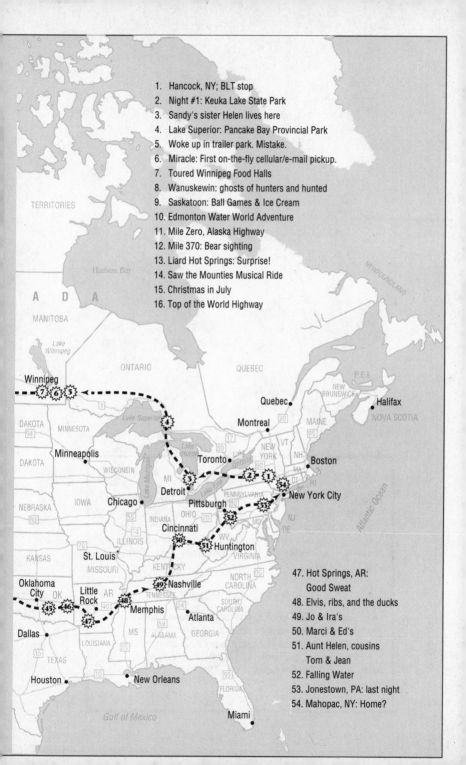

1. Hancock, NY; BLT stop
2. Night #1: Keuka Lake State Park
3. Sandy's sister Helen lives here
4. Lake Superior: Pancake Bay Provincial Park
5. Woke up in trailer park. Mistake.
6. Miracle: First on-the-fly cellular/e-mail pickup.
7. Toured Winnipeg Food Halls
8. Wanuskewin: ghosts of hunters and hunted
9. Saskatoon: Ball Games & Ice Cream
10. Edmonton Water World Adventure
11. Mile Zero, Alaska Highway
12. Mile 370: Bear sighting
13. Liard Hot Springs: Surprise!
14. Saw the Mounties Musical Ride
15. Christmas in July
16. Top of the World Highway

47. Hot Springs, AR:
    Good Sweat
48. Elvis, ribs, and the ducks
49. Jo & Ira's
50. Marci & Ed's
51. Aunt Helen, cousins
    Tom & Jean
52. Falling Water
53. Jonestown, PA: last night
54. Mahopac, NY: Home?

FIRST WE
QUIT OUR JOBS

How One Work-Driven Couple Got
on the Road to a New Life

Marilyn J. Abraham

A DELL TRADE PAPERBACK

A DELL TRADE PAPERBACK
Published by
Dell Publishing
a division of
Bantam Doubleday Dell Publishing Group, Inc.
1540 Broadway
New York, New York 10036

Library of Congress Cataloging in Publication Data

Abraham, Marilyn J.
First we quit our jobs : how one work-driven couple got on the road to a new life / by Marilyn J. Abraham.
p.   cm.
ISBN 0-440-50757-X
1. United States—Description and travel.   2. Abraham, Marilyn J.—Journeys—United States.   3. Career changes—United States.
I. Title.
E169.04.A28   1997
917.304'92—dc20   96-33579
CIP

Printed in the United States of America
Published simultaneously in Canada
February 1997
10 9 8 7 6 5 4 3 2 1
BVG

For Sandy,
the master of change

Contents

1

The End

My eyes drifted across my office. Beyond the elegant gray and maroon art deco furniture, bookshelves filled with the national best sellers for which my firm was famous lined the walls.

Outside were the other immense limestone buildings of Rockefeller Center. Surely this was the most coveted business address in the world. Despite the sixty-plus years since the complex was built, its architecture and decorative art felt fresh and inspiring. It was always exhilarating to walk through the lobby of NBC, with its massive murals.

As I thought about my surroundings, I felt myself floating out through the window, into the fresh air, observing the scenes I knew were there. A few stragglers still ogled the empty set of the *Today* show down the block. Around the corner a dozen or so skaters caught the last days of the season at the famed ice rink as cheerful flags fluttered gently.

I heard the muted ring of my phone and the efficient sound of my assistant's voice. In the beautiful spring morning light, the moment seemed a snapshot in some future album of how work once was. Even the dust was suspended in air, as if waiting for something to happen.

*   *   *

When my boss took the seat across my walnut desk to go over some routine matters, my mind reentered my body and snapped to attention. I focused intently on the business before us. We discussed the upcoming list of books we were publishing and which authors would need special attention. I updated him on our new staff members, pleased to report that they were all catching on quickly. He agreed. A few other odds and ends were reported back and forth. I was glad everything was running so smoothly. As he was rising from his seat, about to go into another meeting, I said, "Oh, yes, there's one more thing."

He sank back into the chair and eyed his watch.

"I'm resigning." My heart pounded in my chest. I hadn't planned to break the news yet, but I couldn't hold it in. The reverie of the past few minutes dissolved into panic, as if I'd suddenly found myself on the crosstown bus without clothes on.

He sank back into his seat and looked at me, head slightly to one side, clearly indicating it was my turn to say something.

"I don't have another job—it's nothing like that," I stammered, not wanting to offend him, even if I'd already stunned him.

"It's just that we—Sandy, my husband, and I—well, we want to have a life. We thought we might do something different. In a small company. Maybe even move. Take a trip first. You know, that old after-college-cross-country thing." I was babbling. But I was also making sense for the first time in a long time.

After a few moments expressing my desire to leave everything in the best possible shape, my boss left to report the news to his boss. I once again looked at the beautiful day outside my window and smiled, knowing I'd soon be out there.

* * *

As I left the office that day, I knew I was not dreaming. I was living my dream. My corporate days had ended.

2

Making a Life

After fifty-two combined years in the corporate fast lane as executive vice president and editor-in-chief respectively, my husband, Sandy MacGregor and I decided to cash out, review our options, set some new goals, see what was over the horizon. The process of deciding to do this was both slow and fast. It began with a shock. One afternoon Sandy appeared in my office looking pasty. His hands were shaking, he was sweating profusely. I was afraid he would die. Then he told me the news. He had just been forced to resign, several months shy of his twentieth anniversary with his firm. Like many other people, in similar situations, we found ourselves numb with disbelief that this could be happening to him, after many years and much dedication. I wanted to make sure it could never happen to either of us again. Our perspective on life was given a major tilt.

The mornings immediately following the news were stilted with routine. Sandy still got up early, put on a suit and tie, grabbed his briefcase, and sailed out the door, brave and robot-like. It pained me to watch the man I loved merely go through the motions of living. Instead of going to his office, he spent his days at an out-placement center sending out his résumé, making phone calls, trying to sound cheerful. While he searched for a job, he simultaneously started looking into what it would take to buy into a small publishing company. After all those years in megacorporations, my husband yearned to go back to a small town and be part of a community. The idea of owning some-thing, creating something that was ours, grew on us. With amazement, I watched him progress from burned out to fired up over a period of six or seven months. We developed an idea of working together, in which we would split responsibilities ac-cording to our inclinations—which, luckily, were very distinct. Sandy had no interest in editing or design, while I would rather eat pins than read spreadsheets.

While Sandy continued to look for a job, I continued work-ing, assuming our lives wouldn't really change all that much. A broker friend began sending us information on various compa-nies. One in New England seemed ideal. Although the town was tiny, it was near a university, a major medical center, and several ski areas. I glibly admitted to the fair possibility of life after Manhattan there for me, a girl born and bred on that lovely island. After all, in addition to all the quaintness you could handle, there was one ethnic restaurant, a bookstore, and a movie theater less than thirty miles away.

After seven months of searching, Sandy got a job offer in New York. While the idea of having our own business still held our dreams, it seemed irrational to turn down a concrete position. The company was big enough to be challenging, small enough to be personal, and young enough to be fun. Publishing books for the children's market seemed a cheery way for him to re-trieve his balance. Sandy once again put on the suit and tie, picked up the briefcase, and went to work. This time it was in a charming brownstone, and he had a bunny on his business card.

The notion of being in his own business, however, stayed with him.

*   *   *

Sandy's story had involved a rapid rise on the financial side of the business world. He first learned the ropes at the Ford Motor Company in his hometown of Dearborn, Michigan. Then RCA recruited him to come east, where he got involved in launching the first modern telephone system in Alaska while the new pipeline project was getting started. His monthly trips to Anchorage and Fairbanks were a heady experience. His next assignment was to develop business plans with a book company owned by RCA. Ultimately, he was seduced into publishing full time and loved it. His areas of responsibility included running the day-to-day operations of his company, which was cited year after year as one of the hundred best companies to work for in America.

All that began to change when the chairman, Sandy's mentor of many years, was forced to resign and a new man came in above him. What followed was so incredibly predictable, it could have been lifted directly from the pages of a bad novel. As they say in those opuses: It was only a matter of time, the handwriting was on the wall, his goose was cooked, the gig was, literally, up. It seemed that no matter how hard he worked or how devoted he was to the house he'd helped build for twenty years, he would always be seen as part of the old team, the wrong team. Over a period of four years, I watched his natural enthusiasm stilled and his joy in going to work squelched. It was no longer one of the hundred best companies to work for.

*   *   *

My résumé was that of a typical baby boomer. My seventy-six million cohorts and I had had entire school systems enlarged to accommodate us. Radio stations completely revised their playlists to appease us. We emboldened each other to wear skirts that were shorter, hair that was longer, as we gleefully outraged our parents. I went to Woodstock, at least in part, to see if my father could take it. Testing limits is part of growing up, I later learned in Psych 101. Then we graduated from college, got rid of Nixon, our nemesis, and thought we would make business-as-usual obsolete.

A funny thing happened to me on the way to the office: I became ambitious, a word I was too modest to use, but the feeling sprouted anyhow. Joining the workforce in a low-paying position at a glamorous publishing company suited my approach/avoidance attitude perfectly: I got to do all the work, but I hadn't sold out because I was hardly being paid. Soon work was all I did. Suddenly the same father who had worried I would spend the rest of my life stringing love beads called to complain that I worked all weekend and took too many manuscripts home with me at night. Working thrilled me: I met famous authors, dined with agents, predicted trends and best sellers, acquired books that became national favorites, and adored my colleagues. We traveled in a pack and cheered each other on. Promotions came, elevating me from assistant, to assistant to the editor-in-chief, to editor-in-chief in a mere fifteen years.

By the time I was being paid well for my talents, oddly enough, some of the charge had gone out of the air. I had the privilege of working for the best companies, the brightest people, and with tremendously talented writers. Yet mergers, acquisitions, and the reshuffling of both staff and authors from house to house created a sense of upheaval and disquiet in the industry. Huge conglomerates were blamed for depersonalizing a very intimate business. Layoffs made everyone edgy, and the continuity that had kept us together disappeared. I mourned the departure of great colleagues. While I survived several reorganizations and the eventual dissolution of my division, I felt miserable when I was told to let several members of my staff go. When Sandy lost his job, I lost my stomach for the whole thing. Suddenly my hippie roots were beginning to show.

*   *   *

Until that moment we looked like a head-on portrait of a two-career couple who had achieved a high degree of corporate success. We were overworked, stressed out, high-strung, short-tempered, and had too many things to do and not enough time to do them in. Now we were forced to blink, to look at our lives in a three-dimensional perspective without the familiar grounding of Sandy's job. Everything started to look unhinged and askew to us. Clearly we were no longer in control of our lives. Perhaps things had gotten out of whack a lot earlier and we had just been forced to stop and notice it.

How had it come about that our life was so out of our hands? Why were we living this crazy life anyhow? Was it really that insane? Wasn't everyone busy, booked, and berserk? (If I hadn't been so busy editing all those self-help books over the years, maybe I would have picked up more knowledge of time and stress management from them. I also should have been thin and rich by now, I figured.)

I flipped through my calendar and my mind to review the life we had created for ourselves. I had to admit we had chosen it for ourselves: no one swooped into the bedroom every morning and commanded me to get to the gym by six forty-five so I could read *The New York Times* and *The Wall Street Journal* while I biked before my breakfast meeting. After that there would be six to eight meetings, appointments, interviews, and personnel reviews each day. Thirty to forty phone calls was normal. Lunch with an agent or author was the only way to talk over a new project without being interrupted. Dinners were good for that as well, and maybe we could squeeze a friend or two into the party. A week like that would not have been an especially busy one since neither of us had gone on a business trip. For a while Sandy would go to England frequently, often for just the day. On weekends we would go to our house at the lake, where we would more or less drop, limp and lifeless from exhaustion, in front of Barbara Walters and Hugh Downs—if we could stay up that late. By the next day we pulled ourselves together to garden, do minor repairs, work on a few manuscripts, read a batch of proposals, review some financial reports, entertain friends and family. That was our so-called life.

One day, after he was working again but still fantasizing about his own business, Sandy did some calculations. He told me that if we sold the lake house, trimmed our restaurant and entertainment expenses, and quit recreational shopping, we would have enough put by that we wouldn't have to work for a year or so. We'd still have the New York apartment I'd had for over twenty years. The place in the city was small, about nine hundred square feet, but it was secure and in a neighborhood we liked. A chilly feeling settled over us. Had we been pushing ourselves, putting up with increasingly pressurized situations, allowing our working time to absorb our life like a black hole, in order to support a house? It was time for a little life review.

It was a nice house. On a lake. A little more than an hour from the city, full of charm and light. But it was just a house. It was our major asset. It was also, in this unadorned scenario, our major burden, complete with a big mortgage, hefty maintenance costs, and mega-tax bills. Our other obligations were minimal. Our kids—that is to say, Sandy's kids—were in their late twenties and financially independent. My parents were in their eighties and fiercely independent in every way. Struck by a bolt of lightning as in a cartoon, the little bulb over my head lit: I wanted to make a life, not just a living. If selling the first house I'd ever owned was the financial linchpin for making that possible, I would have to consider doing it.

For months the fantasy of leaving the city for that little company in New England grew. We imagined how perfect a life it would be: We'd be within driving distance of New York, near family and friends; we'd rent a cozy old place there, sublet our city apartment, and sell the house. As I tried to open up my mind to the possibility of living somewhere other than New York, however, panic set in. I had gone to college in New England but came home as fast as I could. After graduate school in New York, I had tried living in my aunt's beautiful 1827 farmhouse in Vermont. That lasted one winter. I ran back to midtown screaming something about boredom and mud. The population of the town we were thinking of living in was the same as that of our apartment building. I figured I was either in deep denial or just plain old-fashioned crazy. We made an offer on the business.

Now, on a bad day at work, I had my secret life to keep me amused. I pictured my overwrought colleagues tumbling over icy moguls on the slopes near our new home. I mentally threatened late authors by banishing them to the barn to milk cows if they didn't produce manuscripts on time. Maybe I was just losing my grip. Sandy's excitement grew and grew. Having grown up in suburban Michigan, he'd never been a hundred percent happy in a Manhattan apartment. The idea of living in the country, where he could have a workshop and a place to park the car that didn't run four hundred dollars a month, really appealed to him. I was, in the words of a friend's mother, a place bigamist. I could never decide to opt for one over the other. I'd grown up in a Manhattan apartment and loved the thrill of the city, the energy of midtown—though my happiest memories of childhood all seemed to have taken place in the country. From the time I was eight through most of my college years, I spent summers at various camps, which I adored. Tasting the outdoors was not the same as trusting it, however, and I continued to feel more sure of which subway to take than which wild berry to eat.

I was happy at our lake house on weekends and on our outdoorsy vacations, but living in the middle of the woods on a full-time basis would be something else again. It seemed to me that in order to make this kind of megaleap in business and in life, from huge corporation to tiny mom-and-pop shop, from being several feet from my nearest neighbor to, possibly, miles from the next person, required some adjustment. We would need a kind of transition period sandwiched between the life we'd known and what was to come.

*   *   *

A trip, perhaps? What better way to relax, to readjust the little gray cells, as M. Poirot would say. A trip would be just the thing, we agreed. A space between two lives. Our fantasy life was getting richer all the time. With the offer on the company pending, we came home at night and mapped out routes for what was still just a make-believe trip. *Let's go to Michigan and visit your sister. We really have to get to Colorado and visit with Marianne and Timm. Shirley and Bob are dying to show us their new place in Santa Fe. You know, I'd really love to see Alaska, after all those business trips there. Wouldn't you love to go back to Jenny Lake? Don't you think it would be fun to follow the fall some year?*

The scope of "the trip" grew from a little jaunt to something transcontinental. Alaska became our goal. Sandy had been there eighteen times on business, seeing mostly airports, offices, and hotel rooms. He always wanted to go back, and I liked the idea of driving as far as we could on the continent. It wasn't easy finding a map that showed the entire continent contiguously, however. For the most part, Alaska and Canada were lopped off, relegated to tiny "detail" maps that featured every fireplug and pit stop in Nebraska and Iowa but allowed no way to plot a drive to Fairbanks. Useless for our north-by-northwest getaway. In my atlas Alaska wasn't even granted the dignity of an entire page, sharing space instead with the cities of Arizona. When we finally found a continental map, I was surprised how vertical it was. I always thought about our orientation horizontally, east to west, New York to L.A. A leftover, perhaps, from school days when we were coached in theories of manifest destiny and westward expansion.

Looking at the map, I still wasn't satisfied. Something was wrong. Where were the roads? The lower forty-eight was loaded with steady blue lines, bold red lines, gray, black, dot-and-dash lines. But up where I was looking, there was a lot of white space and a few pale squiggles. I felt sure someone had forgotten to print all the roads: there hardly were any. As I read about accommodations, I became more confused. Where were the hotels? What about the cute B&Bs I'd anticipated? I broke out in a rash, remembering the time Sandy had picked up a case of armpit crabs in a lousy motel. We didn't think a series of "clean rooms, shared bath, $24.00" would suit us for what was quickly evolving into the trip of a lifetime. The alternative seemed equally ridiculous: We could rent an RV. As Miss Piggy would have said, "*Moi* in an RV? *Non!*"

Even though it seemed unlikely in the extreme that we were "RV types," on a lark we did a little research. The rental costs for a lengthy trip like ours were absurdly high. Were we nuts? What difference did it make how costly RV rentals were? We had no intention of ever being in one. It was absurd to even think about it. Us in an RV? How would we ever get room service? If, however, someone wanted to travel round trip from New York to Denali National Park, what would be the best way to do it? Surely we could find it! It became a game with a challenge. The trip took on a life of its own. From all the information we could get our hands on, it seemed traveling in a motor home was, in fact, the best way to go. One would have a good bed, clean private bathroom, and home cooking at all times.

It seemed like pure silliness at first. How could we tell our sophisticated New York City publishing cronies that we were getting excited about the idea of traveling in an RV? We'd never even been in one, knew nothing about them. But we fed the growing dementia and furtively started looking at them. Like sneak eating, we went sneak RV-looking. As we went farther and farther afield to find dealers (they did not share lots with Audi, Volvo, Lexus, and those guys, we found out), we became intrigued with the possibility. RVs (recreational vehicles, motor homes, not trailers, we learned) were appealing homes on wheels. We eventually visited with dealers in five states, comparing designs, engines (how wonderful to have a husband who used to work for an automobile manufacturer), and other mechanical features. We test-drove school-bus-size vehicles on small country roads. No special training or licensing was required. My first time at the wheel, it was snowing. It was just like picking up a rental car at an airport, I thought. The layout of the instrument panel was a little unfamiliar, the rearview mirrors and the seat needed some adjusting. But it was easy to drive and felt nice and heavy on the slushy road. The salesman assumed I'd been doing this for years. If only he'd known.

When we got home, we called our RV-owning friends in Toronto, Gordon and Kathy, and grilled them. We learned the lingo, figured out that, if we ever owned an RV, we would want an "A" class, bus-front style, because they offered great views. If we ever bought a motor home, it would have to have a spacious bathroom. Obviously, in the unlikely event we purchased one, it would have to have a queen-size bed that we could walk around so that neither of us would have to crawl over the other to get out of bed. In the living room we preferred a couch to barrel chairs, and of course, we would need a dining banquette. Amazing how many opinions we had about something we barely knew existed.

*   *   *

And then, six months after Sandy lost his job, I got sick. Not life-threateningly, just a four-month bout with pneumonia, bronchitis, laryngitis, and any kind of bug that caught me. I couldn't get myself together and felt it was an enormous chore to do most anything. My staff and boss were very understanding, but there were three hundred books a year for which I had direct responsibility and another four hundred with which I was involved. Missing any time, discussions, meetings meant losing a few threads in the fabric of daily life. I cut back my office hours to half time, got call-waiting at home, had my mail messengered to me twice a day, and canceled all my holiday plans.

I recovered, but sadly, during that same period of six months or so, others didn't. Charlie was my wonderful funny neighbor with whom I'd gone through sporadic periods of jogging. We'd compare notes about the latest diets, though neither of us would ever be accused of being slim. The summer before, however, Charlie had miraculously turned svelte. Though he looked handsome and healthy, for some reason I held back from asking him which diet he was on this time. He died of AIDS at thirty-eight. Joan, my cousin's best friend, died at forty-nine of a rare stomach cancer that, the doctors determined, she had probably picked up while she was a volunteer in Thailand. My dear friend of twenty years, Jane, who had left the rat race years ago to build and run a bed and breakfast in Kauai, Hawaii, died at forty-nine of colon cancer. A colleague died in her sleep of an aneurysm, another was found dead in her kitchen at fifty-one by a friend when she didn't answer her phone while home with the flu. Then Sandy's ex-wife died at fifty-three of kidney cancer. It was an ironic death because it also set us free from a lifelong commitment to alimony payments. Suddenly, but sadly, it was a burden no more.

I was no stranger to death. When I was fifteen, my mother had died after five years of battling cancer, an event so colossal, it seemed to remake all the atoms in my universe. It separated me for all time from those who had not known death at an early age, those lucky ones who thought life went on seamlessly, painlessly, until we quietly slipped away under some prim granite headstone. After that, my world was made up of those who knew and those who didn't. I didn't begrudge them their innocence, but rather steeled myself against the time the next death would strike in my life. Aunts, grandmothers, uncles, family friends, a cousin my age, even my shrink had died.

But this latest onslaught was something else. The combination of these deaths coming so close together, all the people being our age, had a major impact on us both. My thickened layer of self-protection couldn't separate me from my own frailties. We had always suspected we were mortal, but this was a wake-up

call for the comatose. Emotions rose to the surface. Maybe the
notion of enjoying life while we still had time wasn't a frivolous
one after all. We'd have to have been in a trance not to recognize
that we were at a moment in our lives when we had the opportunity to recast our goals, to reinvent new lives that would suit
our future, not our past. What were we working for? Wasn't
being together more important than anything else? Were two-
week vacations really worth the price of being apart all day long
for the other fifty weeks? Were all those meetings and deadlines
and making someone else's bottom line look good worth barely
having the energy to click the remote control on weekends? The
more we talked, the more it seemed we were maintaining a
lifestyle we couldn't enjoy because we had to work so hard to
maintain it. We were both exhausted physically and emotionally.
It seemed to me that after years of seducing authors, cajoling
agents, pacifying bosses, and coddling colleagues at breakfast,
lunch, drinks, dinner, and the office, I just wanted to be quiet
for a while.

*   *   *

Meanwhile, the seller of the company in New England
wanted to know more about how we'd improve the business.
We took this as a positive sign and went back to discuss it face
to face. It was exciting to come up with these plans together.
Meeting with a group of eight at the home of one of the principals, Sandy and I laid out our ideas. Afterward we felt the meeting had gone very well. Our rhythms and attitudes about
working coalesced. Our desire to work together increased. We
discussed the fine points of our offer with our broker, who set
to work negotiating.

Heading home, we felt confident our plan was falling into
place, though on some level it felt like make-believe to me. The
principals even seemed agreeable to a closing six months off,
allowing us time to take our decompression trip. Elated, we
stopped in at every RV dealer along the way, comparing prices,
mechanical features, and interior layouts. With a list of prefer-

ences now in hand, we called the dealer nearest the lake house and asked if he had anything that matched our needs. He told us to come right over. On the lot he showed us a 29' 10" used RV. It had been a rental and was one year old, with 30,000 hard miles. It had a huge front window, a queen-size walkaround bed, and the right furniture and layout. On each side of the bed was a good reading light and a night table. The floor plan allowed for two sets of interior doors—one to close off the middle from the front living area, the other the back bedroom. This created a good-size bath/dressing area in between. It was a lot like a boat, where stowage space is cleverly taken advantage of everywhere. The shower would provide ample hot water for hair washing, and whether plugged in or by generator, there would always be electricity for a blow dry. The living-room sofa was comfy, and the dinette benches and table provided good space for eating, letter-writing, and trip-planning. The stereo sounded fine, the pantry was ample, and the kitchen reminded me of the one in our New York City apartment, only the views were much, much better. We took it for a drive. It was quieter than most we'd been in, and it handled well. It was way past closing time on a Saturday night when we got back to the dealer's office. We talked about the features, we talked about the future. We could have walked away. Instead, we put a one-thousand-dollar deposit down on a Winnebago Brave. Brave indeed. On Monday we quit our jobs.

Our bosses were stunned, our friends cheered, our colleagues scratched their heads and wondered when their turn was coming. Our families were great. I had learned long ago to tell my father something worse than what was actually going on, so the reality wouldn't seem nearly as bad. By the time we told him we were just quitting our jobs and going to Alaska for the summer, he was relieved. It was better than buying a cattle ranch in Australia or some other tale I'd spun out along the way. In fact, he wanted to know whether he could join us for a few weeks. Other people were simply speechless. Were we rich? they wondered. Were we ill? they asked. Neither, we replied. People said we were brave. I thought about that a lot, how it was perceived as bravery to take charge of one's own life. Maybe so. To us, at that point, it felt as if we were doing the most natural thing in the world in order to save our lives.

*   *   *

Memorial Day weekend was rainy and damp, muting the expectations of summer hopefuls. We were deliriously happy. Friday had been our last day at work.

Writing out the check for the motor home had been easy. It was about the same price as our car. Getting it home was hard. It was twice as long and three times as high as a sedan. The parkways between the dealer's lot and our lake house forbade large vehicles. The streets were old, winding, narrow, and shoulderless, with tree branches flopping in from both sides. Very inhospitable to large vehicles. I suddenly had new respect for truck drivers. As Sandy drove the RV home, I trailed him in the car. Now and then I had to close my eyes for an instant when he tried, with his usual impatience, to pass a bus. He hadn't accepted the fact that he *was* a bus. At one point, I saw the road ahead narrow even further and dip under railroad tracks, leaving very little headroom. I held my breath. Would he fit? Sandy suddenly pulled over into a parking lot, the same thought crossing his mind. Jumping out of our respective vehicles, we eyed the situation. There was no sign indicating a height limit. School buses must come through here, we reasoned. Off we went, automatically ducking a little as we went under the tracks, arriving home without incident just as it got dark.

Sandy and I spent the weekend sprucing up our old house and fixing up our new motor home, trying to add a natural fiber here and there to a world that featured only the synthetic. Placing our favorite Amish quilt on the bed made it homier. As Monday evening came around, we were still busy affixing hooks and curtains and were pleased to see the sun trying to break through the mist. Instead of cursing the fact that the weather was improving just as the weekend was ending, I was simply happy to see the sunshine.

It felt incredible to be free. It was the eve of the first day of our new life. Not since 1955 had I awakened on a Monday morning without a hint of regimentation in sight. Weed the garden? Okay, when it cooled off. Cook dinner? In a bit. Have company? Anytime. Hit the road? Ready when you are!

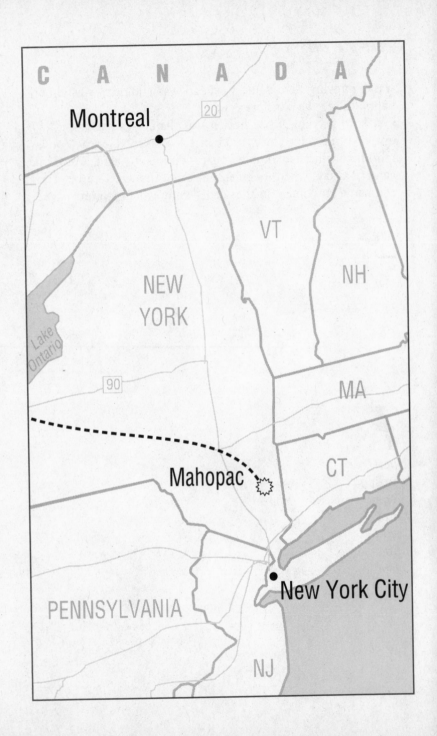

3

Motor Home
& Garden

First, the bad news. We didn't get the company in New England. It seemed they had gotten cold feet about selling. Sandy was more disappointed than I was, but we were both certainly let down. Now what? We had no jobs, no prospects. Plan B appeared obvious: Travel at our leisure and look around for other ideas as we went, while our friend and broker, Jerry, kept his eyes open for us in New York. Maybe it would even be better this way, I rationalized. With no new pressures pushing in at us from afar, we could truly be open to carving a new life. We were now working, or not working, without a net.

We continued fixing up our motor home as if it were a new house. Nest-building was something we both had always enjoyed. We bought new sheets and blankets, a toaster oven, a shower curtain, and lawn chairs. Friends in Texas, Jan and Dean, no kidding, sent a portable gas grill so we could barbecue under the stars. The interior design motif was simple: unbreakable, washable, and portable. Fabrics were by Rubbermaid, Velcro, and that great god of the outdoors, Gore-Tex. Being good little consumers, we found a catalog of all kinds of wonderful things for RVs and their owners. On our doorstep appeared Pop-a-Plate, a handy paperware holder and dispenser; Hide-a-Spice, perfect for compact undermounting; and a garbage sling with a self-contained roll of one hundred plastic bags.

I guess there really are boy and girl genes. Sandy hooked up the CB radio we'd been advised to get, wired in a better light over the couch, and got all the speakers working. I sewed some heavy denim into blackout curtains for the bedroom windows and skylight so we'd have some darkness in the Alaskan summer nights. Sandy tackled electricity like Thomas Edison and I blasted through sewing, ironing, and replacing those curtains in no time. (The reverse would likely have ended in fire either way.) He packed his favorite tool (an electric screwdriver), and I packed mine (a folding 1,500-watt hair dryer). I didn't worry about finding the next best seller, nor did I miss the queasiness about needing to outperform last year's sales. Sandy never once complained about our lack of budget or executive committee meetings. The cherry tree in front of the house, which had failed to bloom the previous year, was lush with vulgar pink blossoms. A new life was dawning.

As we busied ourselves with the details of trip and travel, we tended to our current homes and the details of organizing their care in our absence. The garden would have to be watered, the mail picked up in both places, bills paid, and emergencies covered. We tried renting the house for the months we would be away, but the short lead time worked against us. In addition, we struggled with what to do with Pete and Norm, our adorable young Scottish fold kitties. Sandy had brought them home to me at Christmastime, when I was feeling so rotten. They'd cheered me up and assumed I would always be around to play with them. Norm (named by the breeder after Stormin' Norman Schwarzkopf, with his striped chest and indelicate walk) and Pete (unacceptably named Lord Byron by the breeder, we had renamed him after our catman friend, Peter, who introduced us to the breed) were housecats. The thought of losing them on the road was more unbearable than leaving them in someone else's care. Luckily we found Ann and Joe, who would temporarily adopt our guys into their large household of nine. No kennels for these felines. It was off to cat camp in New Jersey.

Peeling off the layers of our responsibility—no cats, no homes, no mail, no bills—after years of managing complicated lives and many people, was heaven.

* * *

The prospect of living a pared-down life felt totally comfortable—with one exception. It seemed vitally important to both of us to figure out a way to maintain contact with our friends and family. My parents—my dad, Gerard, and my stepmother, Martha—were close to both of us. We talked almost daily. We spoke with Cindy, Sandy's daughter, and her boyfriend, John, regularly and were in touch with son Alex and daughter-in-law Fiona in Austin weekly. And we had great friends who meant a lot to us. Traveling without an itinerary, how could anyone reach us if they needed to? The answer was e-mail. We began the great quest for electronic nirvana like babes in the woods. It took a while before reality caught up with our imaginations.

We thought e-mail would enable us to be totally free—driving through canyons surrounded by snowcapped mountains, unencumbered by society's demands—yet able to reach anyone anywhere in the world with a few keystrokes. Not.

One guy tried to rip us off for fixing the "power problem" with our laptop. Guy number 2 did it for nothing, over the phone in twenty seconds. We needed to buy a modem for cheap. No one on the entire East Coast had it. Called a mail-order house in Oregon, got it overnight. Brought it to nice man number three to install it. Got a commercial on-line service. Installed it and signed on all by myself. What a genius. Any six-year-old could have done it. Next step in the getting-on-line-for-the-future department was making the on-line service (which was to be our only way of connecting with the world for four months) work with our brand-new high-powered cellular phone. Sandy dubbed this period "my life on hold." Whenever he made gargling/strangling noises, I knew that some other techie or operator techie wannabe (a major subclassification of careers, I'd discovered) had put him on hold yet again. The problem: Our computer/modem/on-line service would not speak through our cellular phone line. The phone guys said it was the modem, the modem people said it was the computer, the computer manufacturer said it was the phone. And there was nothing, I mean nothing, more frustrating than being on hold at the edge of wireless liberation. (We briefly considered going back to work at this point, in order to have our in-house tech support staff back. We took deep breaths and sat quietly until the feeling passed.) Why, I wondered, did getting wired, wirelessly of course, require the patience of Job and the tonality of Elizabeth Taylor in *Who's Afraid of Virginia Woolf?*

After two and one half days of being on hold and discussing configurations, baud lines, setups, and how many megs of RAM we had (all words I'd never heard before), Sandy finally seemed to have either (a) gotten lucky and made it through to the on-line help service more than fifty percent of the time, or (b) actually found someone who could tell him what to tweak how, or (c) figured it all out for himself, something he was very good at.

Finally we went to see some humans at a place in Manhattan that specialized in our kind of computer. Incongruously located on the fifth floor of a tenement building, it was a high-tech sweat shop. In a long narrow room with windows at the far end and a row of double-sided work stations down the middle, scruffy-looking young men sat huddled over their desks. For a moment, in the filtered light, they looked like Talmudic scholars puzzling out the mysteries of life. Then I blinked and saw the Nike T-shirts and Yankees caps. We shuffled in among the waiting throng and eventually met Gabe, a junior at NYU. He fixed our various boo-boos in about three or four minutes, cleaned up the keyboard and screen, inscribed himself in our fax modem address book, and sent us on our way. Nirvana at last, electronically speaking. I half-expected a lollipop for not crying.

*   *   *

Preparations for the trip continued, as did the talk about us. We were told we'd regret quitting our jobs. Friends looked at us and, with hands folded like well-meaning rabbis, said they understood what we were going through and implied we'd get over it. We were asked, separately, if one of us was ill. Colleagues wondered if we had job offers elsewhere. There was gossip I'd been fired. There were rumors I was pregnant.

One piece of chatter made its way back to me, attributed to a woman we knew whose cracks generally bested Dorothy Parker's. In a discussion of the comings and goings in our notoriously gossipy industry, the recent death of a colleague was covered, after which our forthcoming four-month trip in an RV came up. Comparing the two events, the wit quickly commented that I had clearly made the worse choice.

People were amazed that Sandy and I wanted to be "cooped up in that thing" with each other. It may have sounded corny, but we loved each other and thought of ourselves as best friends. I had waited till the little hand was just about on forty before I said I do, five years earlier. I had not made my choice of mate easily, quickly, or lightly. He had been through a difficult marriage and divorce. At first it had been truly terrifying to have someone in my life full time. Sharing a whole life, closet space and everything, after four decades of being single wasn't easy. But it did come together, with some attention to details. I liked him better than anyone I knew. He loved me enough to let me be myself, down to the details. (I loved to sleep late, and even though he was constitutionally incapable of doing the same, he guarded my sleep like a mother bear.) One final important piece of the puzzle: We were always there for each other, even after some pretty bad behavior and rough times. After dating a wide range of disappearing unreliable types, it was a shock to my system that Sandy was always there for me. When I was growing up as an only child, I always had this recurring fantasy: On a Saturday or Sunday morning, my parents would surprise me and have a friend there for me to play with when I woke up. Turned out it was Sandy.

Every couple has rhythms, and ours tended toward doing a lot of things together. We had not spent a weekend apart by choice since we married. We had a great deal of respect for each other's ideas and desires. On the surface we were opposites: short and tall, blonde and brunette, Gentile and Jew, midwesterner and easterner, Mother's ancestors signed the Declaration of Independence and first-generation American. We were, however, eggmates, identical twins, where it counted: We were an even match in the brains department, had the same dreams and the same sense of humor.

We were not afraid to spend time together, and both of us tolerated quiet very nicely. Whether people were trying to plant seeds of dissent between us or were truly mystified or concerned baffled us. Perhaps they didn't find the same peace in their lover's arms as we did. Maybe there was an advantage to marrying late: We still had the fire. Something we noticed lately was, we enjoyed being with couples who enjoyed being with each other, who relished each other's victories and admired each other's strengths.

In a last-ditch effort to keep me on the job, one of my author friends, a psychologist on the West Coast, called Sandy to advise him of the dangers of being in such constant close proximity to his wife. He warned him how relaxed I would be, how my body tension would disappear once the continual stress of deadlines was eliminated. He predicted an inordinate amount of affection from me, resulting ultimately in my demanding ridiculous amounts of sex. Sandy couldn't wait to leave.

The leavetaking was the culmination of a process that had begun on the day we made the down payment on the RV, the thousand dollars that changed our lives. We had started verbalizing the possibility of a major adventure in January; on April 8 we put the deposit down; on the tenth (the ninth was a Sunday) we resigned, giving seven weeks' notice to ensure smooth transitions. We then had a month to organize ourselves and say our good-byes to family, friends, and neighbors before the July 1 departure. Although we were ready a few days earlier, we stalled. Why not take off earlier than planned? Who were we kidding about traveling with abandon if we couldn't even abandon the idea of leaving on a particular date? There was one big reason and one little one to wait. June 30 was my dad's eightieth birthday, and I wanted to be with him. Second, the camp bus always left on July 1, and this year, for the first time in thirty years, I was going to be on it.

* * *

Twenty-nine days after we left our jobs, Bob and Helen came over for dinner. Bob had been Sandy's mentor, boss, and friend. I was crazy about both of them. It had been, literally, a month of Sundays of guests and farewells, so longs, good lucks, and good-byes. We'd had dozens of send-off meals with friends and last suppers. We saved Bob and Helen for the end, knowing that as my surrogate in-laws, they'd have some words of wisdom to impart. They climbed out of their car, took one look at the RV, and admitted they found it difficult to understand why we thought it would be fun to go off in a Transue for four months. A what? Transue. Explanation, translation, please. Years ago, they said, when visiting one of their sons in camp, they had seen one of his friends' parents arrive in an RV. It was such an unusual event in that crowd, they all took note. From that day on they called RVs Transues, after the family who drove one. The transue. Transue. The Sue. Susie. It stuck.

After looking over our Transue and the stacks of maps, books, and electronic devices we'd assembled, Bob imparted the following: Did we know the difference between a Jewish good-bye and a British good-bye? The British leave without saying good-bye, Jews say good-bye and never leave. Leave now. Enough good-byes. He was right.

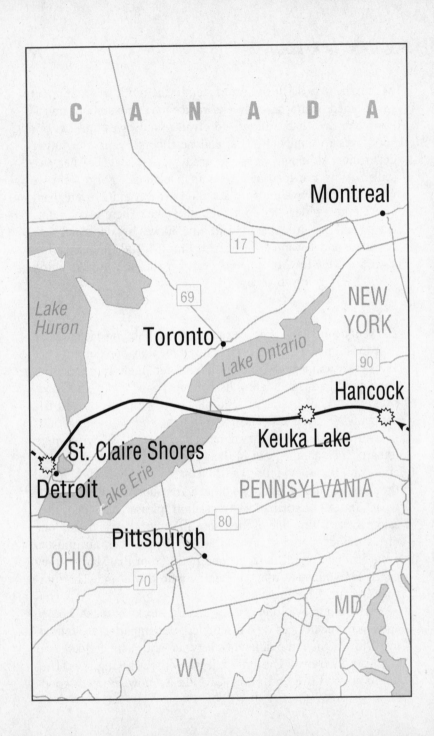

4

Crossing the River

We left shortly after nine on a perfect July morning. Gerard and Martha were there to see us off, my dad grinning hugely as he waved and hollered, "See you in Anchorage!" (After getting over the shock of our defection from our jobs and from the Northeast, *his* fantasy to join us for a couple of weeks had turned into a plan we heartily endorsed.) Our neighbors, Alice and Ronald, came by bearing lots of funny little gifts, including a pair of fuzzy dice that we immediately hung from the rearview mirror. We were not taking any chances in the luck department. Sandy maneuvered the Sue up our narrow driveway and down the winding lake road. After half a mile he pulled over as best he could. We looked at each other and smiled. The RV was so wide, one of us had to get up in order to touch, so I climbed over and we hugged. It was a big moment, starting off on this adventure. We needed a quiet moment to reassure each other and wish ourselves bon voyage. Neither one

said it out loud, but we both knew we were leaving life as we
knew it behind.

I was glad I wasn't driving, even though the driver's seat had
been retrofitted so I could reach the pedals. Lakeshore Boulevard, a grand name for a narrow winding road, was not meant
for large vehicles. We reminded each other that the school bus,
oil truck, and moving van fit, so we must too. We stopped at our
local gas station and made the owner very very happy by loading up on fifty or so gallons (the tank held seventy-eight). Heading across the Hudson, the river that had always marked home
to me, we were truly on our way. As we aimed toward the
Northwest, I scanned the familiar radio stations. Our CB radio
crackled with voices of truckers from other parts of the country.
I couldn't understand a word they were saying. They all seemed
to mumble in a language not quite English. It was like listening
to a two-year-old with all the right inflections on the verge of
speech. I named the generic truckers Nasal Nose and Marble
Mouth.

Our first stop was Hancock, New York, in the bend in the
elbow near Pennsylvania. I had memories of summers spent at
camp near here. Those were times of great independence, away
from the close scrutiny of parents and the restraints of a city
childhood. I learned about sports and nature and friendship and
boys here. Making out on the bus on the way home from bowling on Tuesday nights had been an educational experience. I was
pleased and surprised to see that the town had not disappeared
since the interstate had diverted travelers away from its main
street. In fact, it seemed larger and healthier than I remembered.
A major parade, a few days early in honor of the Fourth, went
by just as we arrived. As we worked our way through the celebration, I kept looking for Kandyland, which had been the local
sandwich shop in my day. I had fond memories of the place
because they provided contraband white chocolate and BLTs
that we sneaked back into camp. To my delight, it was still there.
Even the short-order cook stood at her post, just as I had left
her, hair net and all, nearly thirty years ago. The mahogany

candy counters looked pretty beat up, and the whole place needed a paint job badly. The menu over the soda fountain was still the same, though the prices had gone up some. The only change was the addition of several video games, which were, thankfully, still at the moment. Sandy looked suspicious as I led him to a booth. We ordered the fondly remembered sandwiches and diet Cokes. When they arrived, I understood at once the concept of "you can't go home again." These BLTs were basically Miracle Whip on toast. Gobs of the stuff I hated with a little bacon, lettuce, and tomato. I nearly wept with disappointment as I wiped the stuff off our sandwiches with a napkin. As I daubed away the goop, I apologized to Sandy for the lousy choice of a lunch spot. We left without even taking a bag of the white chocolate. It had probably been sitting there since I'd left the last time. You can't go home, or at least back to camp, again. Back on the highway we made a pact to eat more homemade meals.

One of the few reservations we'd made for the trip was the first weekend at Keuka Lake State Park, in upstate New York. Since it was the Fourth of July, we didn't want to risk being locked out. In midafternoon we arrived at our large grassy campsite. First thing we had to do was get level. We were told that, when parked for any length of time, the RV had to be level in order to keep the refrigerant flowing properly. For an extra two thousand dollars, we could have had hydraulic equipment installed to do this at the push of a button. We had decided to do without the expense and use a level and a couple of two-by-tens under the tires. With a little teamwork, it was easy. After achieving level, we pulled out our awning, beach chairs, and icy sodas. We felt very pleased with ourselves. This RV life was good.

We couldn't lounge long, however. We had a date to keep. We'd come this way to be with Dick and Ellen, who were staying in the area with their friends, Bruce and Gail. Sandy and Dick had known each other since they were tiny—a funny thought since I only knew them as adults. It amused me to try and picture these two balding guys in their fifties as Little League sluggers or dressed up for Halloween. Ellen and I had hit it off right away.

Last time we'd been together, for Dick's birthday in March, Ellen and I had made a huge batch of Sandy's late mother's famous (in some circles) fried cakes. I'd always heard Dick, and Sandy's sister Helen, rave about these doughnutlike treats. In fact, Helen had once sent me the recipe. I'd never known my mother-in-law, but as an odd kind of touchstone, a snippet of her life, I kept her recipe in my wallet. It was a small point of contact with her. There was a notation that she'd gotten it from a Mrs. Thompson. Helen passed it on to me, and Ellen coaxed me into using it for Dick's birthday surprise. An all-girl daisy chain.

In Katie MacGregor's somewhat scratchy handwriting, this was what it said:

Fried Cakes

    1 cup mashed potatoes (about 2 medium)
    1 cup white sugar (1¼ if fried cakes are not to be
      sugared)
    2 tsp. lard
    ¾ cup milk (scant)
    2 beaten eggs
    ½ tsp. salt
    2 tsp. baking powder
    1 t. cinnamon
    1 t. nutmeg
    pinch ginger

Add sugar and lard to hot mashed potatoes. Add other ingredients and enough flour to handle without sticking. Cook at 375° F.

That afternoon, Ellen and I proceeded to make the dough until the two of us were a nice shade of dusty white, as was most of the kitchen. Since she had seen the finished product before, she directed the forming of the dough into shapes. We spread more flour on the counter to keep the circles from sticking as we laid them out. I heated oil in a wok, the closest thing I had to a deep fryer. First, we dropped in one ring and watched it closely. It floated gracefully to the surface, puffing itself up in the process. Ellen removed it with a strainer, ripped it in half, and grinned. She assured me this was indeed the way a Grandma MacGregor fried cake was supposed to look. Sensing victory was ours, we charged ahead. In assembly-line fashion Ellen carefully picked the soft circles off the counter and passed them over to me to slide into the hot grease. As they were done, I scooped them out and Ellen dusted them with sugar. She passed, I plopped and scooped, she dusted. Pass, plop, scoop, dust. A little like Lucy and Ethel in the chocolate factory. By the end of the afternoon, we were crusted in flour, grease, and sugar, but we had a huge pile of tasty fried cakes and the solid base for a lifelong friendship.

Now I looked forward to seeing Dick and Ellen and to what I thought of as a transitional few days. We would be with friends, but not wrapped up in work conversations. With these folks you could always count on a good sail, a good laugh, and a good meal. Gail and Bruce turned out to be incredibly generous hosts. A parade of adults and kids hung around their house for four days and nights. We picked up a rhythm of cooking and feasting, biking and napping. The lake looked inviting, but it was too cold for all but Ellen, who seemed to live by the theory that if it wasn't frozen, it was swimmable. We admired her, but she found herself alone in the water as we soaked up the sunshine onshore. Playing all day came naturally, and much to our surprise, so did camping every night in the RV.

Summer is supposed to be a special time, a time when life slows down a little and chores can be abandoned in favor of play. The way our lives had been going, however, we had felt none of this relaxation in years. There never seemed to be enough "down time" to just do nothing or swing in a hammock and read a book. Since we both had had sales meetings to prepare for in August, we usually postponed vacations till the week before Labor Day. By then we were usually beat. We crammed in as much as we could in those trips. We planned every stop, reserved every hotel, and sometimes made restaurant reservations six months in advance. Determined to get as much as we could out of these holidays, we didn't allow ourselves to sit around. Summer had been getting away from us for years, it seemed.

As the weekend at Keuka Lake drew to a close, we watched fireworks over the water from the campground. Bruce and Gail had already gone home for the evening. We toasted marshmallows over the fire and made s'mores by squishing them between graham crackers and chocolate slices. Dick and Ellen drove back to Rochester to prepare for work the next day. Sandy and I cuddled up under our quilt for a cold night at the campground. This year, we would recapture summer.

* * *

In Michigan we stopped in to visit Helen Martha MacGregor, my sister-in-law. Once upon a time in this country, Helen must have been a very popular name. Especially in Dearborn. Sandy's aunt, his mother's sister, was named Helen, and his sister was also Helen, as were Dick's sister and mother down the block. In order to differentiate among them, Sandy's sister was known as Helen Martha, Dick's as Henno, and Katie's sister was Aunt Helen. That was fine until Sandy's kids started calling their aunt Aunt Helen, and it got confusing again. Now we refer to her as sister Helen. (My friend Marianne had an aunt Helen who was really Sister Helen, Mother Superior, but that's another story.)

Our sister Helen was something else: a ball of fire, a whirling dervish, an elementary school principal who ran those kids into the ground each day. And they adored her. She attended all their sports competitions and baked cupcakes for birthdays. Not your ordinary principal. Never one to let the grass grow, she was mowing it as she waited for us to arrive at her home outside Detroit. Never mind that we had driven four hundred miles that day, there were plans to keep, things to see, places we were expected. We parked the Sue at the curb and brought a few things inside. It already felt odd not to be sleeping in our own bed, but Helen insisted it would be weird to sleep in the street. She probably had a point, we thought, and in any case, I wasn't about to argue with the principal.

She had the next few days and nights planned with activities. On a break we accompanied her as she did some errands. As we strolled the aisles of a megastore with her, it occurred to both Sandy and me that we needed absolutely nothing. We had more than enough clothing, plenty of food and books. There was no room for a twelve pack of paper towels, and we had no use for mulch. What would we do with the large (17.5-pound) box of detergent that did 120 loads? There was a peculiar sense of freedom and relief as we sat outside on a bench in the sun while Helen lined up at the cashier.

When we got back to the house, we took the opportunity to plug into Helen's phone line and pick up our e-mail. As it turned out, the chain of events required to actually do this cellularly, while we were mobile, was something akin to having the planets all line up to form a figure eight on Thursday at noon. In fact, we hadn't been able to make it work yet, though our phone bills would prove we'd tried. We were happy to take advantage of an old-fashioned phone jack. Getting mail from home, even though we'd been gone less than a week, was a thrill.

* * *

Just as I found it hard to picture Sandy as a little boy, it was difficult to see the face of a young woman in that of Mrs. Sherman. Round-faced, wrinkled with laughter, and squinting to see anything at all, Mrs. Sherman, Sandy's father's partner's widow, was the last one left of a foursome. The men, who had been roommates in college, became partners in a small architecture firm. The women became best friends. The couples played bridge and vacationed together, gathered at one home or the other for birthdays, Thanksgiving, and Christmas. The Shermans, who had no children, became as close as family to the MacGregors and their children. Mac and Katie MacGregor died in the 1980s, Phil Sherman passed away the year before. Mrs. Sherman wanted to take "the kids" (that's us, at ages forty-five, fifty-three, and fifty-seven) out to dinner at the nearby Botsford Inn. It was the one place around older than she was, she joked. She felt comfortable in the low-ceilinged dark Revolutionary War–era pub room. She enthused about our trip. We ordered dinner and drinks, Mrs. S. having her daily Manhattan. While we ate, she told us of the time she and Phil went to Alaska in the 1960s, shortly after the Alcan Highway opened to the public. Our trip there would be quite an adventure, she assured us. I marveled at this seventy-odd-year friendship as it enveloped us, the next generation.

When we got back to her apartment, Mrs. Laurellen Sherman wondered what she should do with all her old travel photographs. We had no answer for her. I wondered about ours, those taken and put carefully in binders, and those to come. I guess we did these things for ourselves, for in the end no one would care. That should be enough. Still, I felt terribly sad. We took each other's picture together with Mrs. Sherman and knew she would live on through at least one more generation of trip albums. She hugged and kissed us good-bye and wished she could come along.

*   *   *

We headed north through Michigan. On the way we stopped at Higgins Lake to visit with Dick's parents. At ninety-two, Doc and Helen Arnold still spent summers at the lake house that Sandy's father had designed for them thirty-five years earlier. The house had often accommodated their own family of six, the MacGregor four, and various other kids. Everyone learned to sail, some took up racing, others were designated cheerleaders. There were always wet kids and dogs around. Their eleven grandchildren were already busy creating plenty of great-grand-children to spend summers to come at Higgins. The night we visited, Mrs. Arnold cooked us a delicious hearty high-cholesterol dinner and offered up eggs for breakfast. We scratched our heads in wonder at their contrarian health plan and declined in favor of black coffee. Being with them reminded me of the sense of community that their generation had had and that ours seemed to have missed out on or let go of in favor of job offers or other opportunities elsewhere. These families had been friends for more than sixty years. My husband's face was in their family albums, his antics recorded on their old eight-millimeter films. I had never known my in-laws, but the past few days brought me very close to being with them.

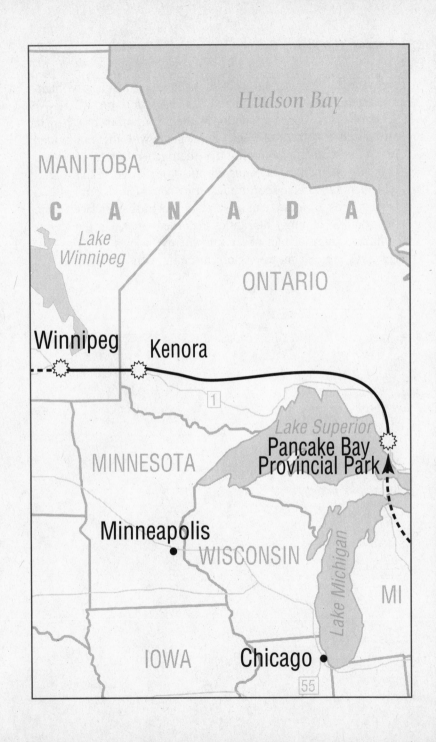

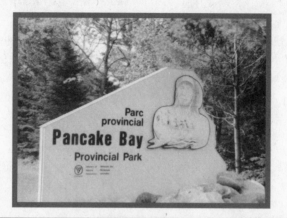

5

Superior

hree months to the day after I resigned my job, I awoke
in my own bed in my traveling castle on the Canadian
shore of Lake Superior, the original Gitche Gumee. I
lifted my eyes to see my wonderful smiling husband, one of
those gifted friendly-in-the-morning types, as he handed me a
freshly brewed cup of coffee. We spent lots of time loving each
other, holding each other, playing adult bunk games, and revel-
ing in our good fortune. The ability to have time, energy, and
desire on days that were not weekends or national holidays was
thrilling. We had time to be childlike, to play, to wonder at
nature and at our good fortune at being in a place this beautiful.
All things considered, I'd rather be here than at, say, a marketing
meeting.

We were on our own. Visits were now a thing of the past. No
more friends or family would dot the way ahead for many
months. Before we left home, we had wondered about, and

worried about, what kinds of people we would find out in the bush. If we were paranoid about the unknown, our friend Joe had been positive about the unknown: He was certain we should be armed and gave us a 30/30 rifle, along with nine bullets. As it turned out, the people we met at campgrounds were friendly but never intrusive. When we did get to chatting, I noticed it was always one of us who asked, "And what do you do?" That was our tried-and-true-Manhattan-cocktail-party-chitchat line. What else would I have asked? "Who are you?" That seemed a little heavy for a campground icebreaker. Plus, I was really nosy, because knowing what people did, I thought, would help me place them in some kind of hierarchy in my mind. Perhaps I would also get an idea or two for our own future. Gradually I cared less about what they did and more about where they had been and what they had seen. When we were asked how long we had been on the road, the discussion inevitably turned to our having quit our jobs. The reaction was universal: Faces lit up, smiles appeared, we were congratulated for our bravery. Everyone wanted to know how we had reached the decision, how we had known it was time to quit.

As people asked, I began to realize that I'd left more from the impetus of a sensation, a feeling, a need, than because of any nicely formulated intellectual reasoning. I'd known it was time; now I tried to figure out how I'd known. It was the hardest decision I'd ever made, because I had loved what I did. Bringing ideas and their creators to market was an incredibly energizing job. For a long time I learned new things every day. I thrived on the variety of information I had to grasp and on the challenge of making it fly with the public. How had I known it was time to quit? It was time to quit when . . . I think it was when I realized I had already left. Often, especially toward the end, when I was at the office, my mind would drift away from the work at hand. I would be somewhere else, anywhere else. If it was raw outside (and I was lucky enough to be near a window), I would think about being in the country stirring up a big pot of soup. On nice days I'd pack a picnic and go to the beach. True confession time: I was a zombie executive. Just like the pod people in *Invasion of the Body Snatchers,* I could not be differentiated from "regular" executives (if there were any) under most circumstances. But during those major gaps, if anyone astute enough was watching, they could have seen me stirring that pot of soup, sunning on the beach, or—another favorite— sliding over a reef in scuba gear.

The more I tried to sort it out, the more I recognized I'd resented what felt to me like the misuse of time. In a well-intentioned effort to communicate, to keep as many people in the loop as possible, we became slaves to meetings. We had departmental meetings and planning meetings and pre-sales meetings and sales meetings (three times a year in a dark conference room in some great city or island we never got to see much of) and post-sales meetings. Everyone complained we had too many meetings. Suggestions for improving how we did things were welcomed. As a result, we had meetings to talk about the meetings.

At the first of those meeting meetings, someone suggested bringing in food to make it a little more pleasant and to allow people to load up on sugar and caffeine. It was great. Menus evolved from the mundane coffee/doughnut routine to more elaborate pastries, fruits, and a wide variety of bottled waters. When we convened in the afternoon, there was salsa, guacamole, and chips. The next meeting meeting provided the intelligence that we should cancel the food because people had begun thinking of the meetings as all-day grazing grounds, something not to get out of in this lifetime. We could not, it seemed, live without all those meetings that were killing us.

The coup de grâce to all of us poor souls who spent so many of our waking hours in meetings was that the primary conference room was windowless, airless, and fluorescently lit. At the end of some of the longer sessions, we felt dead, we looked dead, and we all pretty much smelled dead. Some of our ideas were none too fresh either. Meetings sucked up time like black holes. Anyhow, into my tenth or so hour in any given week in the condolence room, as I came to think of it, my mind would drift to one of my favorite scenes—perhaps an underwater moment with some electric blue or yellow fish and a tangle of sea grass wafting around me and the crunch of shrimp having lunch instead of being lunch. A little smile would cross my lips, I'd breathe a little deeper, and then I'd rejoin the crowd. But then I'd think: Where the hell are the rest of these guys when I'm at sixty feet? One's probably in France, one's between his wife's legs, one's on a job interview. Who knew. I was sure of one thing: At any given moment when that many people got together in a nasty room for that much time, only half of them were really there—the rest were out of our minds and somewhere else. Finally, I simply recognized it was time for me to actually be somewhere else.

*   *   *

Sandy and I adjourned our kind of morning meeting and got up. The weather was turning cooler, it looked like rain, and we wanted to get some exercise in before the storm. We decided to bike along the lake to the town of Rossport, Ontario, eight kilometers west. Kilometers were great, we discovered. They gave us the illusion we had come much farther, much faster. The only problem was the word. Too long and clunky. Years ago, on another trip, we had shortened it to *clicks*. As we rode the eight clicks, a headwind picked up, making the way tougher. These huge inland lakes were like seas: When it was calm, they seemed harmless, but in bad weather they were fierce killers. It suddenly seemed more like November than July as I buttoned my summer shirt up to my neck and wished that it had sleeves. At the far end of town, we saw what looked to be a cozy inn, a neat Tudor building with geranium-filled window boxes. What an oasis for the chilly, hungry traveler.

Leaving our bikes on the lawn, we raced inside to the welcoming lobby, where we met the American owner. We asked if lunch was available, and he showed us to a table by an open window overlooking the lake. We promptly closed it and asked for hot coffee. The warmth of the place and the brew were perfect. We ordered the specialty of the day: house-caught-and-cured lake trout. While we thawed out, the wind gusted back and forth across the water, leaving herringbone ripples and whitecaps behind. It was a lovely day to be inside. Platters of cold smoky fish arrived, garnished with chunks of sharp cheddar cheese, crunchy vegetables, slices of hearty brown bread, and various condiments. We attacked our meal, making sure to sample every combination of tastes. By the time we finished, we were delightfully snug and full. Now we had to contemplate the unpleasant notion of biking back.

As we dawdled over more coffee, the bill arrived. Even though lunch was delicious and we were paying Canadian dollars (which favored us by twenty-five percent or so), it irked me to have to shell out thirty bucks for lunch. For years, we had both been spoiled by large expense accounts. I thought nothing of having business lunches in midtown that ran to seventy-five or a hundred dollars for two. Now this bill seemed excessive. In part, I had to admit, it was because it was our money and we were determined to be careful with it, but in part because it was, well, just lunch. We reminded each other to eat in more often. I would, however, have killed to be able to hail a cab to take us back to camp. Instead we pedaled ourselves through a penetrating mist.

*　　*　　*

Our time along Superior was idyllic. We were really on our own at last—without either kind of reservations. It was incredibly easy to drive as much as we wanted, then stop when we saw a campground. Many times we had looked at the map at home and read the names of the places we would go. Batchawana Bay. Pancake Bay. They sounded so exotic, almost tropical. In fact, when the weather was good, the water of Superior was much bluer and the sand finer and whiter than I'd expected. The campsites we found were directly on the water, quiet and magnificent. The weather changed from hot and dry to cold and rainy several times, but it was all part of the show along the world's largest lake. Finding places to stay was easier than I had hoped. At the provincial parks it was first come, first served. Wherever we wanted to stay, we'd been advised by a friend to arrive by four or so, in the event we'd have to try elsewhere. As it happened, we were never shut out. I thumbed through the tourist literature while Sandy drove. We ended up in this configuration—Sandy the pilot, me the copilot—about three-quarters of the time. It served both our purposes since he liked driving better than I did and I was a better map reader than he was. Let's put it this way—at least reading while in motion didn't make me throw up the way it did him. That made me the default map and guidebook reader. I didn't mind—I found us great places.

In Canada the provincial parks were beautifully located, clean, cheap, and well kept. Sometimes no ranger would be on duty when we arrived at a campground. A note tacked to the gatehouse told us to sign in on the honor system and drop our money in a slot. Imagine a hotel doing the same, we thought. Later in the evening a cheerful ranger would make his rounds and wish us a good night. I half-expected him to tuck us in as well.

One night at sunset, ten o'clock or so, we took a walk and met a very nice couple from Iowa. He was a high school teacher and coach (I asked). They were off on a fishing holiday. With them was the cutest little eight-week-old yellow Lab puppy named Max. She became the talk of the town. All the campers, most of whom had kept to themselves, circled around this little thing and cooed and wooed and wowed.

Meanwhile, across the way, Sandy observed a man in his fifties pull in on a bicycle, loaded with saddlebags galore. We watched in fascination as he undid the bags, put up a two-room tent, and placed his substantial remaining gear on the picnic table, which, except for the grill, he covered with a tarp against the misty night weather. He was endlessly busy. Sandy's curiosity was piqued. We discussed approaching him. Clearly this was supposed to be a *friendly* trip. Reluctantly I agreed we would make contact with our first stranger, without benefit of adorable-puppy intermediary.

"Hi, how far did you ride today?" we inquired. Blank stare. Not friendly, not hostile. I looked for weapons.

"Did you have a long way to pedal today?" trying again. More nothing. I didn't like this one bit. And they said New Yorkers were cold. Ha! This talking with strangers was for the birds, I thought.

We turned to walk away, when suddenly he sputtered to life, making little grunting noises and gesticulating. Then a flow of French spewed forth. I felt better—at least he was probably unarmed. He also spoke no English.

Unfortunately our French was limited to words like *pâté* and *Brie.* Not useful when discussing travel stuff.

I countered by asking whether he spoke German. *Non.*
Spanish, perhaps? *Non.*

Was he kidding? I wondered. Someone on the North American continent who couldn't even say "cheeseburger"? Clearly he wasn't trying. Annoyed, I thought I must be able to get something out of him.

Suddenly, my road French came in handy. He must know *kilometres;* I scraped the back of my brain for the word for *here.* I was nearly sure it was either *ici* or *oci.* I gambled.

"*Kilometres ici?*" His blank look melted, and a torrent of rapid-fire French spewed toward me. Lost cause; I couldn't think of the word for *slow,* even though it must have been a road word.

Then I barked *"Arrêt!"* stop! His look went from gusto to grim. He bent over and scratched "90" in the sand. Our friend had cycled ninety kilometers. Today? Since the beginning of time? We would never know.

We smiled, shrugged, and said, *"Bon soir."* I was going to take this policy of being friendly to strangers under advisement, as my corporate counselors had always advised me.

The next day I learned some more road French. The speed limit in Canada doesn't just "begin," it "debuts." Much classier, I thought. Now I could have asked the bicyclist where he had started. Foreign travel was so much fun!

*   *   *

The farther north we went, the more difficult it was to get radio reception. By the time we were in western Ontario, one of the big thrills was getting any radio reception at all, even if it was the lost and found report. We played tapes instead or let the scenery speak for itself. The few newspapers we came across seemed to have primarily local news that did not hold much interest for us. While the O.J. Simpson case had a head-lock on the press in the States, the Canadian full-page head-lines concerned the trial of a young man accused of killing his wife and her sister. O.J. was all but invisible. Our interest in the news was in direct proportion to how hard it was to come by. We had a television set but rarely had reception, so we quickly fell out of the habit of tuning in for the morning or evening news reports. Our cellular phone didn't work either, due to lack of reception or incompatible cellular services. (Another surprise about being in a foreign country.) We also didn't have the correct telephone credit card with which to make interna-tional calls. It was astonishing how rapidly we were discon-nected from the modern world.

In Kenora I picked the first loser campground. Ironically it was one of the few places we had reserved ahead. It was right on our way, located directly on a lake, and it looked good on paper. When we checked in, I failed to notice the cases of Bud stacked up against some of the permanently installed trailer pavilions. Vehicles were slotted in side by side, shoulder to shoulder. This was the kind of place we had dreaded when we first considered a motor home. Within minutes of our arrival, I started whistling that Roger Miller favorite, "King of the Road." "Trailer for sale or rent. Rooms to let, fifty cents." This was not the right place for us. For the first time it was also hot at night, and we had to turn on the air conditioner. At least that blocked the sound of someone else's bad music. I half-expected my head to sprout hard plastic pink rollers and my sneakers to morph into mules. Too bad we had both quit smoking—this would have been the perfect place to practice blowing smoke rings. We walked down to see the pretty lake, but somehow the place gave us the creeps. In future, I vowed, I would not pick RV parks with the word *trailer* in the name. I'd rather try the A&P parking lot. We grilled a skirt steak marinated in garlic/chili paste, lemon, and soy. It eased our pain.

* * *

As we traveled, it had become sort of a game to look for bakeries. Everyplace we went, if we looked hard enough, we'd find a bake shop. Some specialized in sweet treats, in pastries, or in pies. Others had perfected doughnuts, crullers, and the like. And much to our delight, especially as we went north, hearty sourdough breads became the thing. Why weren't these places featured in guidebooks, we wondered, along with restaurants and hotels? Wasn't locating a toothsome brownie or a crusty roll important information for the weary traveler? We had in mind to suggest to the authorities that an international "B" symbol should be established—white against a blue field perhaps—to indicate their location in every town, just the way

"H" denotes hospital. We loved good bread and were practically phobic about being stuck with air-injected, plastic-wrapped, spongy, tasteless loaves. In fact, we were so concerned about not being able to find good bread that Sandy brought along his bread-baking machine and a supply of sourdough starter. So far we'd had no need for either and felt a little silly about having them onboard. We generally hunted for a good loaf in the early morning, when they were freshest and we were likely to be able to snag a wild doughnut as well. Since I rarely ate breakfast, I left the doughnuts to Sandy.

But after a night in a trailer park, I woke up with a mean hunger for grease. At Robin's, the Canadian version of Dunkin', I tried the Baker's Mistake. An excellent and indiscriminate pot-pourri of everything: chocolate, cherry, orange, and whatever else was left over, fried and glazed to perfection. Crunchy and sugary on the outside. Slightly greasy as I bit down. Soft and moist on the inside. A road delight for sure. I don't know why, but I thought of the little diet diaries and pocket calorie counters sold at supermarket check-outs. I figured we'd better get out of that town fast before my trailer-park-babe persona stuck. I picked up some gum at the gas station.

*   *   *

On the highway to Winnipeg, cruising at a comfortable hundred clicks, about sixty-five miles per hour. Given our height in the RV seats and the level ground, we were able to see a great distance. I had measured the windshield and compared it with our car's back home—it was a panoramic picture window of fifty-three square feet, compared with a porthole of thirteen. The views were astonishing. We were middle-aged (ugh) easy riders, devouring the road.

We also had our first successful mobile cellular e-mail experience—and just about exploded with excitement. All the pieces we had spent so much time, money, and energy putting together back home *finally* did what they were supposed to do.

We had mail! Lots of mail to read. And all the mail we'd been writing and saving to send got sent. One of our friends coached us, on-line, about off-line composing and reading. It was so exciting to be cruising down the highway, the computer on my lap, flinging messages into space. Meantime this little international ride on the information superhighway probably cost us mucho dinero. But then, our upcoming night at Moose Mountain Provincial Park was about to run us eleven U.S. dollars. We thought that might balance out the phone bill.

Winnipeg (or Winterpeg, as one expat Canadian wag calls it) was very pretty. We were able to quickly find the refurbished old warehouse district, now filled with a glorious food market. It didn't take long to fill up as many bags as we could carry with meats and cheeses, fruit, bread, and all kinds of veggies. The unknown loomed ahead, and who knew when or where we might find real *parmegiano-reggiano,* Brie, or cervelat salami again, right? We stocked up on fresh garlic, as a talisman against bad food. Every nook of the refrigerator was put to use storing these gems of civilization.

After that fruitful stop in cosmopolitan Winnipeg, we were off on Route 1 across the plains of Manitoba. What a beautiful surprise. I had pictured endless vistas of flat dullness that we would want to get through as quickly as possible. Instead, the fields were magnificent carpets, huge squares of yellow, sage green, bold green, blue, and white, making up in multiples for the flatness. It was a 360-degree checkerboard. Helpful signs told us they were growing canola, wheat, barley, strawberries, raspberries, and corn. There were lots of mature trees clustered around farmhouses. Off in the distance Sandy spotted giant loaves of bread. I thought he was just configuring his next sourdough masterpiece, but no—there they were. Upon closer inspection, they turned out to be loaf-shaped hay mounds. Odd but scenic, and I'm sure there was a reason for them.

Instead of finding the plains boring, I became enchanted

with the grain pool elevators that appeared as landmarks along the highway. Most were painted barn red or gray. Wooden, several stories high, each had what appeared to be a silo-type structure attached to a vertically elongated barn or two. Every town had one with its name painted, proudly announcing our location. The radio reported local crop and livestock prices. As we cruised along the divided four-lane road, we were bombarded by battalions of dragonflies that seemed to be trying to cross the road. Instead, they landed up in profile on our very large buslike windshield. They thunk-thunk-thunked against us as they drifted across in swarms. These insect squadrons transformed themselves into something Jackson Pollock would have been proud of.

I took time out from copiloting to do some sit-ups, make lunch, or get us a soda. I learned how to turn the generator on while we were moving so I could microwave popped corn as a snack. From time to time I'd flop down onto the couch and do a little reading. When I drove, Sandy kept the cockpit supplied with diet Cokes, jellybeans, and anything else the captain required.

The road was soothing, almost hypnotic. The slightest hill became a "feature" giving us an even better view. We stopped at a roadside truck farm that sold peaches, nectarines, and cherries. Big signs all over the truck and the table boasted B.C. FRUITS. I hoped that indicated British Columbia and not edible antiquities. The fruit man cut little bits for us to sample. They all tasted wonderful, but we went for the cherries—the biggest, sweetest things I'd ever had. We could eat them only singly since each one filled up our mouths. As our teeth popped the skin, the warm sweet flesh rolled over the tongue, offering up its sugary delights. Rolling along on our summer vacation, we felt that life was just a bowl of cherries after all.

*   *   *

Tip: Don't ever tell your hairdresser you won't be around for four months for another cut. They really take the opportunity to scalp you. In my case I looked like a furry tennis ball—really attractive. And don't believe what they say about it growing back. Mine shrank every time I washed it. Every day I could feel it getting reeled back into my skull.

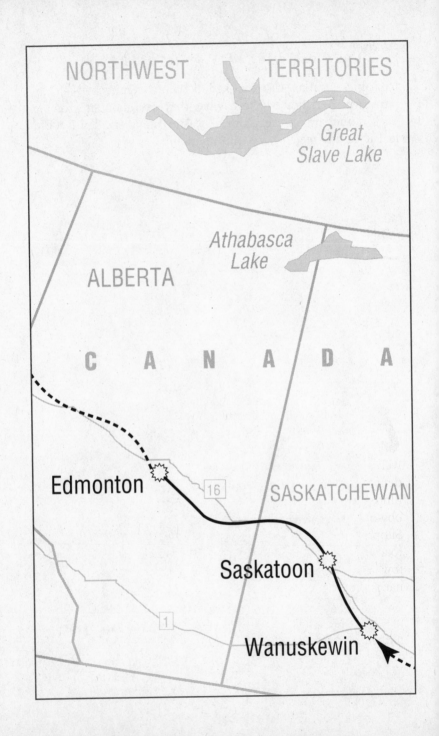

6

Roman Holiday

Bastille Day. Bang, bang. Regina (rhymes with *vagina*) is a classic cow town and sprang up at us out of nowhere. Abruptly, it was just full-blown there. One minute we were driving Canada Highway 1 through barley fields, and suddenly ungainly swan-necked streetlamps lined the highway. Behind them a 1970s-era city appeared. Regina didn't hold any obvious charms for us since we had all the salami we needed. Slipping through it quickly, moving in and out on the main roads—Victoria and Albert—we continued on our way up toward Saskatoon. I loved the place in advance because of its name.

Time rubberized. The trip was making me aware of the silliness of the concept of bite-size time. Time was big. When we nibbled away at it, chiseling out this appointment, that meeting, another lunch date, we had made it small. Now, when we didn't have to parcel it out, time very quickly began to stretch. One afternoon we shopped for postcards. The clerk handed us our change, smiled, and wished us a good weekend. As we walked out of the store, our grins turned to laughter. A good weekend? That meant it must be Friday, we reasoned together. Who knew? Who cared? The division of time into weeks and weekends was an invention we no longer had to live with. I savored that childlike sensation of having a delicious, endless summer ahead.

Boundaries became even less clear as the days themselves lengthened as we went north. Light rarely left us now. We had plenty of time to take a bike ride or walk after dinner, before it got dark. The time zone changes as we went west further increased our sensation that time was no longer a hard fact. Time changed literally, and time changed within us. Our clocks and watches were useless and unnecessary. Their purpose was supplanted by instinct. We quit keeping time. In return, time no longer held us hostage. We ate when we became hungry, not when the clock struck an hour. We slept when we were tired, not when it was dark. And what wonderful sleep it was. No replaying business dramas to keep me from succumbing; no upset stomachs to get Sandy up. As weekends and weekdays blended, our rhythms smoothed out. I no longer had to balance several four-hour nights during the week, when work anxieties kept me up, with a twelve-hour Friday or Saturday night. It seemed I had been a sleep bulimic, bingeing and purging on rest time. Now I consistently slept between eight and nine peaceful hours each night. Sandy settled in at eight.

Only the bigger time, the seasons, mattered. It was summer, and we were at liberty. Morning, noon, and night, and the hours and minutes we chopped them into, didn't mean much at all. We were learning to take bigger bites. The flavors lasted longer.

*   *   *

One afternoon the sky seemed to be rolling evil weather toward us. The buttercup-colored canola fields turned psychedelic yellow as steel storm clouds rimmed the northwestern sky. Looking at the map, our first instinct was to go to the Native heritage park called Wanuskewin, "place to find peace." We slipped off the highway and out of time. Few cars were parked in the lot. Distinctly different from the cultivated land we had been seeing, the landscape looked barren and uninspiring to me. I wondered why the First Nations, as Canadians call Native peoples, thought it special. What secrets could this place of no apparent beauty or even identity possibly hold?

An orientation film was just beginning in the auditorium. We were the only visitors. The narrator, in a mesmerizing voice, whispered, "Wanuskewin," and told of people coming to this spot for six thousand years to herd buffalo and make winter camp.

"Wanuskewin."

The people weren't farmers, they were hunters. It was an ideal place to hunt the animals because of a hidden drop-off in the earth.

"Wanuskewin."

Many beasts were brought together by clever hunters, who then created a disturbance.

"Wanuskewin."

The animals would instinctively run in the direction of what appeared to be open land.

"Wanuskewin."

Instead they went to their deaths over the edge of the buffalo jump.

"Wanuskewin."

This place became sacred to the people, the narrator said, for providing food, clothing, and shelter, all of which the people created from the buffalo. Background voices kept repeating "Wanuskewin" like a mantra. By the time the film was over, I thought I felt a little rumbling of hooves. Outside, the sky still dark, I tried to imagine this emptiness filled with men, women, children, and animals. Warren, a young Cree guide, talked with us. His face was like those in the film: smooth, brown, and wide. He explained that each of the four trails laid out for the public explained a different aspect of the lives of the people who lived here and their relationship to the buffalo, the land, and nature. We followed the trails while the storm went elsewhere. Life as a Plains Indian had not been easy. We wandered around for a short time before heading back to the Sue and the late twentieth century.

*   *   *

In a guidebook we'd read about a Mennonite restaurant in Saskatoon and thought to try it, looking for a fix of butter-drenched noodles and enormous platters of whoopie pies. But the place was closed because of a family death. We hunted for something else that we might not be able to fix for ourselves, doubting with every sophisticated New York prejudice that anything good enough was likely to be found this far from anywhere. In fact we found a busy Vietnamese restaurant and dined sublimely on spring rolls, rib bits, and a tangy hot pot for about seventeen American dollars. It was a delicious cosmopolitan meal, priced right, with free parking and spaces big enough for an RV. If we hadn't been too full, we could have eaten our doubting words.

Not far away we found a campsite at the Gordon Howe Municipal Park, where we caught part of a fastball game. We arrived well into the first game, so the kind, smiling ticket taker waved us through. "Enjoy it!" she called after us, as she turned to continue telling her girlfriend the details of her date the previous evening with a guy she called Lucky Lenny.

As we took our seats, two local youth teams were giving it their all. The *smack* when the bat hit a ball dead-on brought cheers from the bleachers filled with sisters, brothers, parents, and grandparents. Two other teams, warming up for the next game, played a lazy catch in the field behind us. When the next game began, we realized that sitting in the bleachers had somehow made us hungry again. It was not hard to scare up a couple of ice cream cones, which we devoured walking back to the Sue. That night, as we were falling asleep, we were serenaded by a concert across the river. All in all, it was just how summer is supposed to be.

* * *

Saskatoon had been as lovely as the name sounded. Leaving it behind, we continued driving a roughly diagonal northwesterly path across Canada. We had accustomed ourselves to RV living with an aptitude that surprised us. Our world seemed perfectly contained. Living in the RV turned out to be more than just okay, it was grand. I wondered why it was so much fun. Then it dawned on me. It was like playing house. When we were kids, we used to play house in Bennett Park, where a big rock was our "house." Deep gray, shaped like a turtled *Niña, Pinta,* or *Santa María,* it was amazingly complete. Everyone could tell the front from the back by the pitch of the rock—a deep crevice running along one side served as a good place to sit down or a place where meals, courtesy of the Bungalow Bar and Good Humor, could be taken. Afterward, if you were really pooped, you could stretch out along the rear curve and have a nap. Now, forty years later, we traveled along in our land yacht, cruising highways and byways for daily adventure. There was a dreamlike quality to the ease of our lives as we played house in this compact universe. The border between fantasy and reality grew hazier, and I wasn't sure that was a bad thing. True, I felt guilty from time to time that life wasn't painful enough, that there wasn't enough tormenting me, and that the angst that had driven me for so many years might perish. But then there would be another beautiful vista to share with Sandy, or a pleasantly exhausting bike ride, or we'd be surrounded by the rich earthy smell of pine woods—and we'd continue happily playing.

Yet we were about to abandon ship. On one of the many evenings back home spent map gazing, it seemed obvious that we would want a break from being in the RV. In the way that one projects about the unfamiliar by using what one knows, we had come to the conclusion that after three weeks and three thousand miles in an RV, we would surely want to spend a couple of nights in a real bed, with a real bathroom, in a real hotel. We'd pointed to the spot on the map named Edmonton and decided that, since it looked to be the last outpost of civilization we'd see for a while, this was the place to decamp. We read about the FantasyLand Hotel in the West Edmonton Mall. Although the jungle, pirate, and other theme rooms seemed a bit over the top, it sounded like a good location. The parking lot would clearly be able to handle a motor home—an important consideration. Envisioning a sort of attenuated last supper event, complete with king-size bed, full-length bathtub, room service, and all the shopping we could handle, we booked two nights. Though not particularly antsy at this point to leave the Sue, we pictured romance, relaxation, and rapid retrieval of e-mail.

As it turned out, the lobby was under construction, and we had to ferret our way through the mess to the elevator. Upstairs our room was pie-shaped, dark, and totally unromantic. The bathroom was functional, fluorescent, and nondescript. Even with the aid of an adapter provided by the hotel (upon request), our computer's modem couldn't access the phone line, dashing our hopes for news from home. The possibility of room service getting through the lobby labyrinth seemed remote, so we settled on the dining room instead. Looking out our slice of window, we saw the Sue in the parking lot and wondered why we were shelling out $250 to be in exile from her. We were homesick.

*   *   *

Until recently, when it was surpassed by the Mall of America in Minneapolis, West Edmonton was the largest mall in the world. It wasn't just your everyday mall—it was a vacation destination, a resort, a place it took days to explore. Projecting from Manhattan how we'd feel at this point in the trip, it had seemed just the thing. But after being out in the sunshine, hiking, biking, and looking at nature for three weeks, it seemed bizarre to be indoors. Every store ever seen in a mall, plus every catalog shop, was there. Shoppers drifted in and out their doors. We realized how satisfied we were in our mobile bungalow. Despite the fact we had divested considerably compared with, say, our five-closet apartment, we felt amply filled up with things. We had learned a simple new fact of life: Fewer things produce less "thing anxiety." Not needing to buy anything, we looked for things to do. As we wandered around for a while, the sensory stimulation was overwhelming. We decided to chill out and see a movie. After spending a day at the mall, with eight hundred shops and restaurants, a miniature golf course, a full-size ice rink, an amusement park, a casino, a chapel (there's a mix!), several movie theaters, and a submarine tour/aqua show, we fell asleep, exhausted.

The next morning we wanted to leave, but we had to stay. There was something we needed to do. Amidst the carnival atmosphere we yearned for a return to our primordial origins, to the moment in evolutionary time before seduction, when all was naive bliss. Scanning the endless path before us, we saw the sign:

WATERWORLD THIS WAY → → → → →

We followed. Below the level of the earth, a line formed. Money was exchanged for keys, suit, and a piece of drying cloth. Men and women were separated. Down a long hallway an opening in the abyss revealed a meeting of our primeval past and blessedly simple future. It smiled, wore a bathing suit, and hot yellow inflatable tubes.

Welcome to summertime, anytime. This was what we had come for. Check your clothes and troubles at the door. No matter what the weather (in Edmonton, where it could be minus anything in winter, this was important), the swimming here at the mall was fine. The "pool," which had no traditional shape, was entered through a gradually sloping end, giving the impression of being a "natural" body of water. It was the size of a football field, and the water was a comfy eighty-three degrees. Far above us a vaulted glass ceiling revealed a true blue sky. All around, snaking waterslides, some six stories high, spewed forth the adventurous young. At the far end was a whitewater tubing area for wimps like us. And then there were the waves. Just before a set was about to roll, a foghorn blew a warning. Heartlanders sampled the concept that they too might hang ten and be surfers. Whew, just caught a big one! People of all ages just howled with delight as they tumbled over one another. Everywhere we looked, there were smiles. The shopper pods had been broken to reveal giddy, silly, amiable people. Those Romans had known about this part—weren't they the ones who invented socializing in the baths? Bread, circuses, and water—the secret ingredients for a happy mob. Children were loving it, grandparents were too. Everyone got in the mood screaming, laughing, bobbing up and down. Seeing this scene of bliss, we found it impossible to doubt that once upon a time we must have been shrimp.

While we were all having our beach boy dreams, human flies lined up to hurl themselves off a platform over the deep end of the pool. Looking up, we watched as the already criminally happy bungee jumped, to the cheers of the crowd below. Feeling like a little thrill of our own, we grabbed our Day-Glo yellow tubes and went upstairs to the top of the "raging rapids." We plunked down among the twelve-year-olds for a truly mindless whoosh through the whitewater tunnels.

After all that excitement we opted for a little rest and a soak in the hot tub. Later we lounged about on beach chairs reading mystery novels, munching nachos, and generally thinking, Life is a beach, and other brilliant thoughts. While it was odd being in that hermetically sealed bubble for two days in the midst of summer, the water park was divine.

* * *

Fully marinated, the next day we headed out. Back to what was beginning to feel like the real world to us: being on the road in the RV.

7

Mile Zero

Toting our little black bag out to the parking lot and into the Sue, it felt tremendous to be home again. Back in our New York driveway, when we first were fixing up the RV, every time I'd go inside I was a little bit disappointed that it never smelled like home, not like our home smell, whatever that is. Now she did have a homey aroma. At least one of the components of that smell was salami—strong,

spicy, garlicky Winterpeg salami. Every time the fridge opened,
a cascade of eau de salami poured out. Just to make sure we
didn't run out, we hit a supersaver store on our way out of
Edmonton.

*   *   *

CONFESSIONS OF A PROVINCIAL NEW YORKER

I was convinced that no one outside of New York—and possibly a few other urban areas, but I wasn't counting on them—
knew anything about food. The Vietnamese meal in Saskatoon
was an omen that I was wrong, but I assumed it was an exception. My mistaken assumption prompted us to pack, along with
the bread machine and the sourdough starter, sun-dried tomatoes, lots of fresh garlic, dried porcini mushrooms, a little leftover white truffle oil, arborio rice for risotto, anchovy paste and
Parmesan cheese for Caesar salad, chili paste, sesame oil, curry
powder, frozen New York bagels (H&H sourdough, the best),
and a dozen other essentials we feared we would never
find "out there." It went right past me that, except perhaps
for the bagels, none of these things actually came from New
York in the first place, but I was a rube in reverse. What did I
know.

*   *   *

Major comeuppance: The supermarket in Edmonton was
fabulous—especially the produce. Everything from duck eggs
(sold singly) to bok choy and large hands of ginger, to tropical
fruits and a range of berries rarely seen anywhere: gooseberries,
red and black currants, black and red raspberries, strawberries,
and those lovely Saskatoon berries, cousins to our blueberries.
The quality and variety of products amazed me. I had expected
New York to have the best of everything. The world was full of
surprises. We had lots of different salamis to choose from. And
ah, that simple Canadian packaging. Why did the Philly cream
cheese 125-gram box look so sweet, so innocent, and our

eight-ouncer so crapped up? We'd also noticed how Canadian food packaging was blissfully free of what sometimes seems to be excessive, mind-numbing labeling. I know it has its place. I can hear Susan Powter screaming at me now, but surely no one really needs to be told that butter is fattening or oil is grease. Since we had warned and labeled and identified food in America, we had become fatter as a nation. The only assumption I could make was that we were now doing it on purpose! In Canada, Sandy and I could still eat with the ignorance of children, having determined through trial and error and rigorous intellectual pursuit that lettuce was probably better for us than lard, and that fruit was a healthier dessert than cookies. Imagine, all that thinking for ourselves! And along with road French, we were able to add a few words of food French to our vocabulary. My favorite was *guimauve,* a much classier way to say "marshmallow," *non?*

Meanwhile the Sue had her innards lubed and her fluids checked. As New Yorkers, we were always expecting the worst kind of punishment simply for having a car. That's how it was at home in Manhattan, where you had to beg someone to change your oil and let you pay them sixty dollars. I'll bet they wouldn't touch an RV for any money. So before we left home, we'd called ahead to make an appointment for this check-up through the concierge at the hotel. Both the concierge and the nice man at Mr. Lube must have thought we were nuts making an appointment weeks in advance. As it turned out, *we* were a day late for our date, and when we did show up, they were so efficient, we barely had time to shop for groceries down the road before the Sue was all set to go. Paranoid citiots. (That's short for *city-idiots,* as a someone I know once referred to the summer people in his beach community.) We had been concerned about finding places to camp— but this *was* where people camped all the time. Campgrounds were as common as subway stations. If we were in Queens, we'd have had to worry, but not out here in this part of the world!

Back at home, on the road, I put on my favorite garment. I'd always wanted one of those safari-photographer-pockets-everywhere vests. It proved to be an incredibly handy way to carry water, tissues, lip balm, the camera, and extra film. The little tortoise pin on it, a gift from our friends Liv and Willie, was supposed to remind us to take life more slowly. But after three weeks of traveling, counting miles and making time, moving had become our natural state. The stasis in Edmonton bothered both of us. It took some effort to remind each other that this was not a two-week holiday to be devoured but a new way of life to be etched. I hoped we would be able to enjoy each day as we went along and not always be on the lookout for that next place or next adventure.

Passing a golf course/RV park, I chuckled at the combo. More to the point, *it was totally flat out there.* People I knew would say this wasn't golf, it was bowling. Along the road the trees had all been planted, mostly evergreens, giving a little bit of a Christmas-tree-farm feeling. Noting odd town names was a good way to amuse ourselves since I refused to play Sandy's counting-cows game. On the map I noticed Humptulips, Washington, and Mouth of Wilson, Virginia. Sandy especially liked Sexsmith, Alberta, and said what a good trade that would be. I didn't get it, thinking of *trade* as in swap. But I should have been quicker—he meant it as in a profession. My husband wanted to be a sexsmithy. I reassured him he already was.

* * *

Just beyond fifty-five degrees north latitude, the scenery began to get a little hilly and natural, as apparently unplanted trees appeared. After a thousand miles of totally open vistas, our vision was abruptly narrowed to a tunnel of blacktop surrounded by green soldiers standing at attention. It must have been very disorienting for a Plains Indian to come into a forest for the first time. How claustrophobic the sudden limited vision would have been. How strange not to be able to see that straight horizon line that had always separated heaven and earth. It must have been something akin to how we were feeling about our new possibilities. Ahead of us the land spread out again, and I felt relieved, as if the open space had become my familiar too. The dirt was black, and the fields glowed. It seemed as if someone had turned on the sunshine at the edge of the canola fields. Every once in a while an oil well would pop up in the midst of the crops. As we drove toward Peace River, the earth suddenly fell away, and we realized we had been on the high plains, a giant mesa. Below us were three rivers: the Peace, the Heart, and the Smoky. The Beaver and the Cree once made peace at their confluence. Now there was a tea room for tourists in a greenhouse. Across the way the vertically undulating hills gave the impression that if you could rub your hand across them, they would feel like the felt of a pool table, with ridges.

Radio reception, something we'd always taken for granted, was now an increasingly rare treat. When we were able to pick up a signal, it usually didn't last past the town limits. One day the lead story on the news was that the city council approved a new "Welcome to Fairview" sign. I paid close attention to the death notices. It struck me that these deaths had much more immediate impact on the daily lives of the listeners than the obituaries I read in the *Times*. These were neighbors and friends who had died, not cultural icons at some remove. As we traveled, the newspapers, magazines, and radio and television reports I used to gobble up regularly became increasingly irrelevant. At first I'd suffered some withdrawal when we couldn't find *The New York Times* for several days running, especially on a Wednesday. I loved the Living section. I also missed the ritual of reading the Sunday *Times*. But did I miss the news itself? It was the first time I noticed a difference between the two. Information still filtered through to us. It was impossible to escape knowing the large strokes: Bosnia was still in crisis, O.J. on trial, baseball on strike. If something major happened, I figured we would know.

We spent a night in a woodsy lakeside site in a provincial park. Although it was midsummer, it was also midweek and there were few other campers. It was a great relief to be on our own again. After laying in a supply of firewood, kindly provided by British Columbia, Sandy heated up the grill. I nuked an acorn squash (available everywhere, they kept unrefrigerated forever, it seemed) and steamed some rice in an onion soup broth, and when the pork chops were done, I tossed a salad in our homemade garlic dressing. We dined at a picnic table set aside for our campsite under a canopy of trees. After a short bike ride to watch the birds fish in the water, we went back to light the campfire and toasted a few *guimauves*. Now this was real romantic.

* * *

Dawson Creek in British Columbia was notable for being mile zero of the famous (it said so on the sign) Alaska Highway. In preparation for the journey we tanked up. Gas by the liter ran anywhere from 45 to 69 cents, or about $2.30 a gallon. (If you think those numbers are strange, try asking for your cold cuts in grams. I thought only drugs came that way. Or try driving a monster truck at sixty miles per hour—excuse me, ninety clicks per hour—toward an overpass with a sign that says, in English and in French, "Maximum headroom 4.2 meters.")

At the gas station I got out to wash the windows—a very funny sight, I'm sure: a 62-inch woman hanging by one arm on a 137-inch-high truck with a squeegee in the other hand and filthy window water running into her armpit. I noticed the fellow at the next pump also had New York plates—the first we had seen in days. This was exciting. I hadn't sensed any homesickness at all, but there in Dawson Creek I felt an instant kinship, an intimate connection with a guy I had never seen before because of a license plate. His vehicle and ours shared, with only eleven million others, the same kind of tag. Oh, the camaraderie! He nodded toward us and was clearly happy to see a couple of folks from back home too. My blood flowed warmly toward him. Who says New Yorkers aren't friendly?

We immediately struck up a conversation. We were on our way north, I told him, having a great time. He was on his way south and eager to warn us how awful the road conditions were. He couldn't wait to get back home to Manhattan as fast as he could. I withered with disappointment. My soulmate turned out to be a party pooper. After Sandy took out a second mortgage to pay for the gas, I slunk back into the Sue and wondered how I could have so misjudged my fellow New Yorker. As we pulled out of the station, I heard him yelling at us and thought perhaps we'd left something behind. I turned and saw him waving frantically while videotaping our departure. We waved. Maybe he wanted evidence to take to the Mounties when we were reported missing.

The Alaska Highway is the only year-round overland route into the state. Built by the army during World War II to enable troop access to the North Pacific, it is at best a two-lane black-topped road. Often it's dirt and a single lane. From this point until we got to and through Alaska, all the roads were to be referred to by name rather than number. Taking the Richardson? Heading up on George Parks? It sounded much better than taking I-95 to 287 and 87. The roads also had mile markers placed religiously along the way, making it easy to know your exact location, even if you were thousands of miles from anywhere. Our bible in this part of the world was a book called *The Milepost.* It listed every identifiable inch of road, by the garbage barrel here to frost heave there to landmark hotel not to be missed. We knew we were 3,351 miles from home, 1,488 miles from Fairbanks. It was still wild territory here, with very few other roads and fewer towns. We were warned never to lose sight of how much gas we had and how far away the next station was. As we drove, seventy-foot double-length trucks whizzed by us, bringing supplies to the North. Neither of us had ever experienced remoteness before. It was simultaneously calming and thrilling. At Mile Marker 370 we saw our first bear, a little black cub scooting out from a landfill.

I had always thought of roads as sturdy, permanent. When a highway opened, it was forever. Even roads built in ancient Rome, England, and Israel were still intact. The road to Alaska was different. It was always shifting and movable. People and the planet battled constantly about whether that black strip would stay put. Pavement was turf in the war between ice and earth. In a good year a road could go bad in no time. In a bad year forget it. It was a constant process of give and take: People gave it their best shot, and nature took it all back. As we drove farther north, the road seemed insignificant compared with truly permanent mountains and rivers. They were the real bosses of the road crews here. A turquoise river, the Toad, followed along our side for a while, backed up by the stone-faced mountains. The little strip of road was clearly here by their permission. The mountain could eat it for breakfast any day now and wash it down with a gulp of Toad.

We had no radio reception at all, signaling to me that we were as remote as we'd ever been. When we pressed scan, the numbers on the display flashed at us and never stopped. No station featured traffic and weather together on the eights, twos, or any other time up here. When work was being done on the road, however, we had the scoop. The Long Island Expressway or the five in L.A. are not known to get personalized, individual road status reports. Up north, when vehicles have to wait while dirt is being moved, flattened, or graded, each driver hears the whole story and dimension of the work in an up-close-and-personal kind of way. Signs warned us well in advance of a slowdown. We learned to time lunch, soda retrieval, driver switches, and bathroom breaks according to road conditions.

The first time we were approached by a member of a crew, I thought some major calamity must have occurred ahead. Was a bridge washed out? A truck overturned? Were they looking for escaped convicts? Just the road news, ma'am. Friendly (generally also young, blond, and female) road workers would come up to the driver's window and chat. How were we today? How far were we going? Then we would get a description of the project, how long we could expect to wait today, how far this particular job stretched, and where the next bit of work was. Pretty civilized up here in the outback. It helped keep the blood pressure down—a good thing in a place where everyone carried a gun, I guess.

At the edge of a milky emerald lake we stopped for the night. The opacity of the waters in this part of the world was a result of glacial flour—runoff that hauled with it aeons of finely ground rock. It created beautifully colored waters, terrible for fishing. We sidled up to the shore and rolled out our awning. The sky was still threatening, so we decided to go for a hike right away. Wearing our Gore-Tex just in case, we scrambled up the side of the mountain until we had an overview of the campground. The water changed color with the mood of the sky: gray, green, turquoise, black. We watched while a tour bus pulled in, relieving itself of passengers, who relieved themselves in the latrines and reboarded. From our lofty position it was like watching the Keystone Kops moving jerkily back and forth. By the time we got back, we had neighbors. A young couple and their small daughter were pitching a tent. They were on their way home to Whitehorse, they explained. As the rain began in earnest, I was glad not to be in a tent.

* * *

In places the road became very primitive. Pilot cars led caravans of cars, trucks, and RVs through muddy pathways around equipment. Often we wondered whether we were on an old road, a future road, a shoulder, or just something to get us out of the way of the workers. I thought about our usual anxiety in traffic jams, how tense we became. Here it rolled off our backs. We had no appointments, no reservations to keep. Any personal need could be taken care of easily since we were already home. I felt like a pioneer on a wagon train. At night I imagined it was like "the old days." We sat around a campfire and shared stories with those coming the other way: How was the road? How was your weather? See any animals? Conditions varied from smooth and amply shouldered blacktop to dirt and rutted and barely big enough for two cars to pass. Skies changed hourly, and the sunny weather of the plains disappeared. For the most part the clouds were benign. Then one would roll over the mountain behind us and open the floodgates. There was a sense of discovery along the highway. One night we camped next to Judy and Ken, young retirees from Oakville, Ontario, on their way down from Alaska. They were bubbling over with enthusiasm about the Great Land, its beauty and ruggedness. Eagerly they described their trip up the Dempster Highway, a faint dotted line on our map, from Dawson City, in the Yukon, to Inuvik. They also were the first of many people we met who encouraged us to go north from Whitehorse to Dawson in order to take the Top of the World Highway into Alaska. They explained their various routes to us, which glaciers they liked best, and how they had come to love dry camping, being completely self-sufficient. They seemed like sensible adventurers. Taking advice from total strangers seemed as reasonable to us as following a guidebook. A new laissez-faire attitude had kicked in. We were still dubious about the Dempster but leaning toward the Top of the World.

The road was our shepherd.

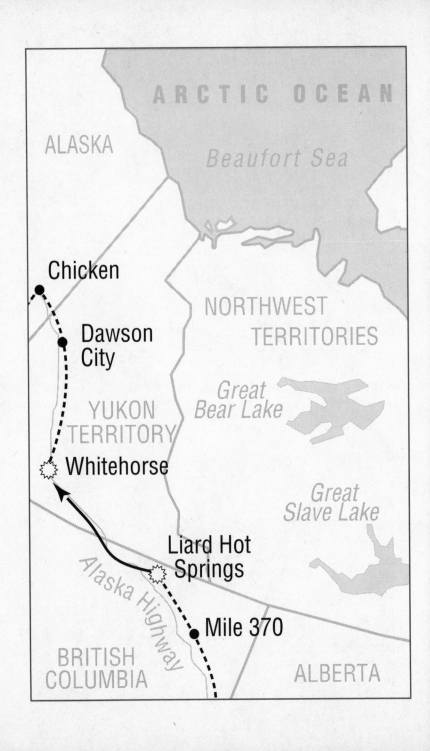

8

Sergeant Preston,
If You Please

After driving the Alaska Highway for many hours on a raw day, we needed to decompress. Our bodies were tired from holding on, bouncing around, and gripping the wheel. Our minds were exhausted from anticipating bumps, calculating distances between work sites, and trying to grasp hold of reality in this foreign environment. We headed for Liard Campground, about 850 miles north of Edmonton, a thousand miles from Fairbanks. Our site had ample privacy, no electricity, and a water pump down the way. Just as we were about to collapse onto our lawn chairs, we noticed something odd. Streams of people—couples, families, clusters of teenagers—were coming out of the woods nearby with wet hair and happy faces. The shower house was in the opposite direction. Grabbing our bathing suits, we decided to investigate.

We followed a trail that led to a boardwalk. Passing through a swamp that looked like prime moose-grazing territory, we hoped for a sighting. These large vegetarians like to feed on water plants and willow bushes, in areas we called moosaurants. No diners at the moment. All we saw were a few birds. Walking on, the vegetation looked familiar but out of place. There were fernlike plants and bushes that reminded me of palms. Then came something that looked like a castor bean plant with powerful thorns. Someone said it was called an Indian club. Everything was very lush and green. Red high bush cranberries dotted the scene. Despite the fact that it was a gloomy day, there was something cheerful in these woods. The parade of wet, smiley campers coming toward us continued.

Half a mile down the path, we came to a pond. Along one side was a wooden terrace and bathhouse. Steam rose from the water, particularly from one end. In various stages of immersion, people of all ages were at play. Evidence of human and animal sojourns to this place have been found dating back thousands of years, making Liard Hot Springs, in my mind anyway, nature's inspiration for Waterworld in Edmonton. We changed clothes and eased into the water at about the midpoint. To our left the pond cascaded over a miniature waterfall toward a cool spot. On the other side the water grew too hot for me, as the temperature rose above 115 degrees Fahrenheit. Once accustomed to a moderate warmth, we felt our aches melt away in the moist heat. We bobbed along from rock to rock, searching for the perfect spot.

A group had clustered near the waterfall, and we joined them. It was becoming easier for me to talk to strangers out here. A word or two about the road, the weather, the water, or the campground would start a simple conversation. It struck us that "what do you do?" was a rare topic of interest, except perhaps to us. But what did people do up here? I wondered. Talking with a couple from Fort St. John, British Columbia, about thirty miles north of Dawson Creek, began to open my mind. Their kids, a boy of about nine and a girl thirteen, played with each other in the water and occasionally came around to listen to the adults. Cathy and Mike, refugees from Vancouver, had moved north to Fort St. John in 1979. They had sensed that their life was more hectic than it needed to be and less fulfilling than it could be.

On the verge of starting a family, they wanted a place where they could grow, along with their children. Cathy eventually decided to take responsibility for home schooling Mary and David, at least through their elementary years. Mike, a pharmacist, wanted to do more than pour, count, lick, and stick. In the smaller community of Fort St. John, he became an active participant in the health and well-being of his customers. The six of us spent the afternoon together lolling in the Eden-like atmosphere of the hot springs. The kids were extremely content, and we marveled at how well behaved they were. Mary, blond and lithe, told me about her favorite books and authors. Her eyes sparkled as she spoke. She confessed she wanted to become a writer. I believed she would.

That night we gathered again, in our living room this time. Over cookies we talked about changing lanes on the highway of life. Although Cathy and Mike had remained in the same province, they were 750 miles from Vancouver. The population in the Fort St. John area was 40,000, though only 14,000 locally. They were both greatly satisfied with their choice and, when they went down south to visit friends and relatives, found the city increasingly unpleasant. In terms of both work satisfaction and overall quality of life for themselves and their children, moving had been a wise move. Cathy was interested to know what books I'd read about Alaska. She tried to be informed about her new territory and enjoyed sharing that interest with the children. She'd read all but one of the titles I mentioned, the name of which I wrote on a piece of paper for her. She said she would check it out of the library as soon as they got home. This wasn't idle chat. Somehow I'm sure she did. In the morning as we left, we drove past their campsite to say good-bye.

*   *   *

We had always planned to go through the Yukon Territory, so getting there was not a surprise. Being there was altogether unexpected. The road sometimes seemed made of Silly Putty, stretched here and there at our expense. The terrain was rugged, wild, and big. As easterners, New Yorkers, we were unprepared for the size of the territory before us. Most of our maps cut off this part of the world as if it were irrelevant: not Alaska, not the developed tourist areas of Banff, Jasper, and Lake Louise in Alberta. The Alaska Highway zigged and zagged back and forth between BC and the Yukon seven times, as if it too weren't sure which way to go, increasing the anticipation of moving through the territory. Eventually we all made a commitment. We had our bearings. We were off to Whitehorse to see the Mounties.

By our fifth day out of Dawson Creek, we had found the rhythm of the road and felt comfortable. We went up with the heaves, down with the washouts, left to go west, straight ahead for north. The sky was gray most of the time, and the air felt noticeably cooler. Shorts sank toward the bottom of the cubby, and turtlenecks floated to the top. Evergreen mountains surrounded us. There were no intersections, no choices, no alternative besides turning around. Signs of civilization were thinning out. Food was harder to come by, and gas a rare commodity. We kept a northwesterly heading.

* * *

I devoured the quiet. There was something very seductive about the isolation. Sandy and I wordlessly agreed to forgo listening to our tapes. My mind was able to tick away its own thoughts. For some time back home I had been feeling put upon by noise both human and mechanical. Mysterious street repairs made in the middle of the night by men with jackhammers kept me awake. When I called my parents, they would inevitably get on both extensions and end up talking to each other or shushing each other while I listened. In meetings everybody spoke and nobody listened. I'd always kept my office door open, a practice I'd learned from my first boss and mentor, Mr. Jaffe. Why was it, I wondered, that people would walk in and talk to me while I was obviously engaged in a telephone conversation? Bad manners? Too self-involved to notice? Talk, talk, talk, blah, blah, blah. Then the noise of the subways, hawkers on the streets in my face, unwanted phone solicitations at home, music (not mine) coming from somewhere, and the television that seemed to turn itself on wherever we were. Thirty years later I understood what my mother meant when, exasperated, she would plead with some unseen spirit in the sky for tranquillity. I too sought quiet. When I had taken up scuba diving and became at ease in the deep, the first thing that became apparent were the incredible fishes and their electric colors. The second thing was the sound. All I could hear was my own breathing as I pulled the air from the tank to my lungs and returned little bubbles to the sea. I loved it.

Now, for the first time, I found that peace on land. We heard only the wind and felt it push our hollow bus around. We called attention to beautiful creatures and sights for the other to see. We made love and murmured against each other's throats.

*   *   *

Whitehorse, the capital of the Yukon, announced itself in writing for many miles before it actually put in an appearance. A modern town of 22,000 in a 162-square-mile area along the Yukon River, it offered anything the weary traveler might desire without any of the complications. The streets were broad, flat, and easy to move about in the RV. We easily found everything we needed: a campsite overlooking the river, a good Chinese restaurant, and a well-stocked bookstore to replenish our supply. Sandy had seduced me into reading mysteries. He'd been reading them for years and suggested I try Sue Grafton and her alphabet series. I started with *A Is for Alibi,* and each town we came to, I now fled like a junkie to my dealer for my next fix. Even though the books had no sequence other than the titles, I made a game of reading them in order and buying them one at a time. (I am also the type who saves the frosting for last.) It was a delightful addiction.

Mac's Fireweed was a wonderful place with a good general selection, lots of local works, and many periodicals. We dove in. I found *D Is for Deadbeat,* looked over the headlines, then declined to pay ten dollars for the Sunday *New York Times* but couldn't resist *Log Homes, Alaska* magazine, *Vanity Fair,* and *People.* Sandy found a book called *Wilderness Seasons,* an adventure autobiography by a young Vancouver couple, Ian and Sally Wilson. Thus armed, we went back to our bungalow on wheels and fell asleep in the lingering daylight.

After a righteous breakfast of coffee, fruit, and cereal, we followed our noses in the direction of our campground neighbor, a fellow in his sixties in a black cowboy hat, fixing an aromatic pancake-and-bacon breakfast outdoors on a grill. We decided to call the guy Curly, after the Jack Palance character in *City Slickers.* Sandy was intrigued by the gizmo Curly was cooking on, which was attached to the RV's propane tank, and went over to strike up a conversation. He learned that the grill was homemade. Not something most folks we knew would think of, since you could buy the things for about twenty dollars. But out here independence was everything. If you could make it, why would you buy it? I was inside devouring *D,* sniffing the bacon, and wishing it were mine. I couldn't make out the words, just heard a gravelly voice. Sandy came in to pry me out. As we rode our bikes down the hill into town, I looked back over my shoulder. Curly was just sitting down to breakfast. I hoped it wouldn't kill him. I was really just jealous, though.

We set out to find the action. Rotary Peace Park, along the riverbank, was the place. Various tents were set up on the periphery for locals to hawk their wares. We picked up a couple of sodas. People had positioned themselves on the grass around the ring. The Mounties were due to perform their celebrated musical ride any minute. After a hundred years of protecting and serving the people of the Northwest, this summer was being spent as a dog-and-pony, or horse-and-horse, show of appreciation. We found spots in front of the bleachers and spread ourselves out, eager to soak up what could almost pass for sunshine. A few rows ahead of us, I noticed a little blond girl and nudged Sandy. "Wasn't that the kid who camped next to us the other night?" Sure enough, small world—when her mother turned around, we waved at each other. The entertainment began with several warm-up acts, including a First Nation singer from over near Burwash Landing. Everyone but us seemed to know where that was. Then came the Mounties—thirty-two red-jacketed riders and their high-stepping, tall black steeds. They strutted and danced with a precision that would have made the Rockettes proud, weaving in and out of formations, into lines and circles, then back again. The sun, as if on cue, came out for real, and the music played all around us. The children in the audience watched with a dedication I'd previously seen reserved only for cartoons. It was a perfect summer afternoon, uncomplicated by modernity. Even a provincial girl from New York City could be content in the Yukon Territory on a day like that.

After the show was over, we loaded our bikes onto the RV and made our choice to head north to Dawson City. We couldn't resist the opportunity to take the Top of the World Highway into Alaska. It was a summer-only gravel road with breathtaking views, we'd been told. Having come this far on the Alaska Highway, how much tougher could it get? we thought. It was late in the day when we made camp at Tatchun Lake, less than halfway to Dawson. By then, it was raining but far from dark, allowing for a quick hamburger grilling on our store-bought appliance. As we sat inside our cozy home, we felt a great deal of satisfaction. It was not the sense of accomplishment of a business deal concluded or a manuscript edited, but a slower, deeper sense of well-being. We were happy being where we were at that moment, not wishing away time until the weekend or anxious to get past a tough employee review. The change of place, the change of pace calmed and energized us simultaneously. Life was simple, life was good.

When the rain stopped, we walked down to the lake and ran into the only other campers in the park. A man and two boys skimmed rocks across the water. Some things have always been satisfying.

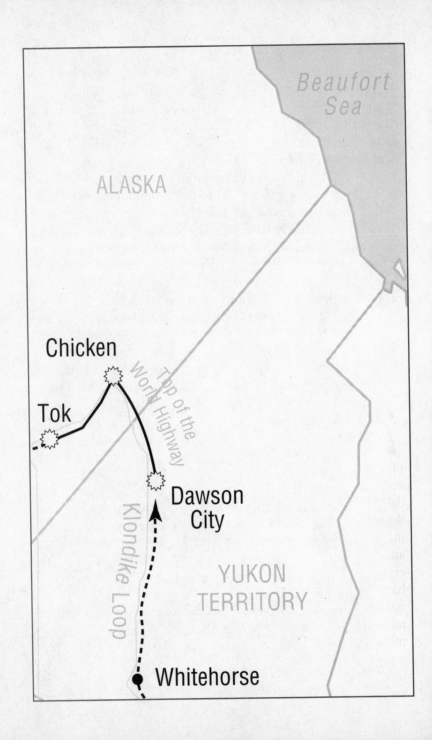

POKER CREEK
ALASKA
ELEV. 4127 FT.   POP. 2
MOST NORTHERLY LAND
BORDER PORT IN THE USA

9

Gold!

The next morning we drove an easy couple hundred miles. In the East we would have measured this in terms of megalopolis distances: New York to Boston, Philadelphia to D.C. At home a trip like that would have been a day's event: getting the car from the apartment house garage (at a daily rate of twenty bucks or monthly for four hundred) out of the city and onto an interstate would have been time-consuming and exasperating. Four hours or so later, after inexplicable and unexplained traffic jams, tense face-offs with anxious drivers, and a pit stop in some grim grimy bathroom, we would have arrived. Arrived to face weaving through another city to our ultimate destination. Hardly a pleasure. That two-hundred-mile stretch back east would have been home to ten or twenty million people and no elk. Here we rolled out of bed and onto a nearly empty two-lane road called a highway. If there were forty thousand people in the province, including tourists, I'd eat my head net. (Everyone had warned us about the, ha ha, state bird of Alaska, the giant mosquito. Thus far we had seen none, but we had those head nets that draped down to your collarbone just in case.) Animals were everywhere: mountain goats, black bears, deer, and elk.

Near lunchtime, as we traveled alongside the Klondike River, the road curved hard to the right. The river merged with the Yukon, and we arrived at Dawson City, metropolis of the North, population 1,852. (The place where the Alaska Highway had started was Dawson Creek. This place was Dawson City. It was confusing. Both were named for George Mercer Dawson, who had surveyed the region for the Geological Survey of Canada in the 1870s. People must have been very grateful to him.) A tiny outpost that had boomed to boast 35,000 residents during the gold rush of 1898, Dawson City had become a decrepit ghost town by the 1950s. From what we could see, Parks Canada was doing a good job revitalizing the town as a tourist attraction. The commissioner's residence, a spiffy-looking yellow mansion with sharp white trim, welcomed us to town. In the summer, cruise ships that plied the Alaskan coast brought visitors up by the busload and kept a steady stream of people at the hotels, saloons, and gambling halls, all of which were required by law to have an accurate period look. In the water that paralleled Front Street, the S.S. *Keno,* an old ship that once brought supplies upriver, was still in its slip but immobilized. The streets were dirt: dust when it was dry, mud in the rain. The western-style storefronts were mostly just that: barnlike buildings with fronts attached for show. We were 4,750 miles from Manhattan, and it showed.

The weather was grim, chilly, and damp, so we looked for indoor activities. There was no movie theater, the gambling halls were closed for the day, and the burlesque show was too. Where were all the tourists? we wondered. We went to lunch in one of the hotels and found ourselves the only guests. Odd. It was the cruise ship's off day, we were told. Not that many people drove here, it seemed. That explained the weird sensation of being in a ghost town of a ghost town. Plenty of amiable staff were available to bring us to our table and provide menus. We chatted with several of them about the weather, which colleges they went to, and how many summers they had been coming up here to work. Though they admitted to suffering from cabin fever, the weather having been exceptionally gray all season, they were happy to talk with us and took good care of us.

In order to cheer up his imported summer crew, the manager decided to declare Christmas in July (it was the twenty-fifth). The dining room featured a fully decorated tree and whatever decorations they could scare up. Candy canes replaced mints as we left. The service was jolly. The burgers, soup, and diet Cokes were superb. It was an altogether successful holiday season as far as we were concerned.

We commented to each other how different this simple dining experience was from going to some fancy "in" spot in New York, where one listened to a waiter give a dramatic recitation of items no one could possibly remember. Upon taking the order, he would have smiled unctuously and said, "Good choice," as if entrée selection were a contest and we were well on our way to winning. As we left the hotel dining room that day in Dawson, we waved at the staff, and they smiled at us and did the same while we hollered "Merry Christmas" back and forth.

* * *

In New York, the capital of culture, we rarely had (or made) time to go to the Metropolitan Museum of Art or any of the dozens of other museums and galleries in New York. It was easy to think of excuses. We were too busy, too tired, too scheduled. There was no place to park. Everything was too crowded. After Christmas lunch in Dawson City, there were no excuses. We headed for the local museum, not expecting much. Inside the impressive brick building, however, we learned about the beauty of isolation. Since we were the only takers, we had a private museum tour, complete with local lore, history, and details of the miners' lives one hundred years ago.

While it hadn't been easy for us to get to Dawson, it surely had been no struggle. I couldn't help but wonder about the stamina of the miners who had come nearly a century ago. By land to Seattle, by boat to Skagway, then over high mountain passes in the deep snow. Each man hauling the required year's worth of supplies with him—about a thousand pounds—in order to be admitted to the besieged territory. One display was a recreated miner's cabin. It was bare in the extreme. It made me cold just to look at its rough-hewn airy walls and dirt floor. Clearly most of the hopefuls had been unprepared for the harshness of the environment. Still photographs of the town showed a bustle of activity difficult to imagine today, even on days when the tourist buses were in. The market area was just like anywhere else, full of buyers and sellers. Movies taken by Edison, jerky and silent, revealed a touching hopefulness in the faces of the men. Despite the hardship and remoteness, they came determined to find their fortunes.

Imagining the swell of excitement created by the cry of "Gold!" we looked at the facts. In April 1897 the population stood at 1,500. By the winter of '98, there were as many as 40,000 souls in the immediate vicinity. A year later it was back to 2,500. The majority were either dead, discouraged, or distracted by other finds. These days mining was still going on around the area, but only on a small scale and when the mood struck. I thought about what Manhattan would look like if it were abandoned suddenly. It chilled and somewhat frightened me that a place could have had such currency, then in a flash be dust again. No matter how impressive the buildings, how important the monuments, how incredible a feat of engineering the roads, the culture and its trappings had just melted away.

I was glad we were not in Dawson City in January, when the mean low temperature was −30 degrees Fahrenheit. It was raw enough in July. I was wearing long underwear and ski pants most of the time. The climate wasn't doing much for our sex life. I had a new sympathy for women who were called frigid. Maybe they were just cold. Even when we turned the heat on and got some of the dampness out, I couldn't get evenly warm for any length of time. Sandy would press his palm against my nose to gauge how I was doing. We both wondered how people lived in this climate in winter. We were eager to get going, to get to Alaska, but decided to hang around to wait for the rain to stop. Since we were about to embark on the road with the best view—so it was said—in the world, we thought we would pick a day when we were able to see it.

* * *

One of the quaint (read: annoying) reminders of the way life used to be in the gold miners' days was the lack of bridges crossing the rivers. In order to get across the Yukon, we had to take the free ferry shuttle service. The only catch was that it was capable of holding only two vehicles at a time. One morning, when the clouds parted, we got on line and waited. There was a sense of excitement among the travelers, despite the iffy weather and the line. As we emerged from our vehicles (many were RVs), sipping coffee together and telling road stories, we found it difficult to know whether it was the snap in the air or the sense of anticipation that was making people hop from foot to foot. At home a wait like this would have made us both crazy. Before long Sandy would have been at the head of the line directing traffic, and I would have been on the phone, returning calls, frantically trying to make use of the wasted time. In the Yukon we both looked around, read a little bit, had some more coffee. After two hours it was our turn to make the crossing. We were on our way. Of course we had been on our way to Alaska all along, but now it was real. And just across the mountains.

The Top of the World Highway runs almost magically from ridge line to ridge line without seeming to dip into the deep valleys below. There are no man-made distractions along the way, only range after range of mountains disappearing into the distance, or the mist, as the weather permits. While we had known the road would be gravel, we hadn't counted on the ruts and the dips that made us slow down to thirty-five miles an hour most of the time. The good news was, this gave us more time to enjoy the incredible views. As we bounced along, splashing mud nearly to our roof, the world seemed to fall away beneath us. Squinting into the distance, we found it difficult to determine where the layers of mountains turned into layers of clouds. Aside from the gravel road itself and those of us on it, virtually no sign of civilization was to be seen. We pulled over at a rest stop so we could take in a full 360-degree view. We looked down on trees, mountain ranges, and valleys. Along the horizon was a sea of sky. All the clichés about scenery taking your breath away came to mind. Perhaps this was permanence, I thought as I pondered the direction our lives would be taking. Towns, cities, and man-made shrines could evaporate and die, just like the people who built them. Sandy reminded me that even nature allowed no continuity—Alaska had been the site of three of the century's ten most violent earthquakes. If the only constant was change, why did we humans seem to resist it so vigorously? Only while we were traveling did changing and accommodating to circumstances seem easy. Maybe we would stay on the road forever.

It was no exaggeration to call this the Top of the World Highway. As we drove west, the concentration of RVs increased noticeably. We began to recognize certain vehicles, creating the impression that we were part of a loose alliance of fellow travelers. Information about road conditions was passed to those coming from the opposite direction. The longer you'd been traveling, the thicker the coat of mud on your vehicle. The badge of courage in these parts seemed to be brown, not red.

We entered Alaska at Poker Creek, the northernmost land

port in the United States. We took pictures of each other, the signs, and the view. A simple little log-and-mud structure at the border was the government building. Ellis Island this was not. Beyond Poker Creek we passed our first Alaskan town. After the gorgeous scenery it was something of a letdown. The community of Chicken, population 37, was supposedly named by the original settlers for their favorite fowl, the willow ptarmigan. However, since no one was sure how to spell it, they gave up and settled on Chicken instead. There was an immediate sense of being on the frontier. The town's facade was rough, and its streets were dusty. We pressed on, declining to stay in Chicken or take the dead-end cut-off to Eagle. Our destination was Tok, a big town with a population of 1,250. We arrived, dripping mud, after a grueling yet exhilarating 191-mile, eight-hour drive. It took as twice as long as New York to Boston usually did, but what a different trip it was.

* * *

We actually got a physical rush from arriving in Alaska, a sense of a job well done, a personal milepost. We found a campground, appropriately called the Sourdough, and went directly to the do-it-yourself RV bath. The Sue was up to her ears in mud. We took turns doing the soaping and rinsing. At first we splashed ourselves and each other accidentally, but we continued with intent until we were soaked and breathless from laughing. Executives are not supposed to do this sort of thing. Parents discourage this kind of behavior in their adolescent children. Hah. What do they know about fun? Finally the RV was clean, we were filthy, and we headed for hot showers, warm dinners, and dry beds.

Later, exhausted and elated, I padded off in my bare feet toward the bedroom.

"Omigod!" I screeched. I felt the distinctly repulsive squishing of icy liquid between my toes. My dreamy mood was shattered. I hollered for Sandy and together we patted down the carpeting around the platform bed. It was soaked. We dismantled the bed and bedding, Sandy using his old reliable electric drill to remove the screws that held the plywood platform top in place. Under it, we knew, was a fifty-five-gallon freshwater holding tank. We inspected it carefully but couldn't find a leak. Sandy went outside to look at the hose that fed the tank from the fill opening. At one place the flexible plastic pipe sat on a piece of unfinished, roughly cut wood that separated the interior of the cabin from the "basement" storage space accessed from outside. It was dribbling. Clearly it had not survived the Top of the World Highway as well as we had. After mopping up as much as we could with towels, I used my old reliable tool, the hair dryer, to blast away some dampness. In the end we had no choice but to sleep on it.

The next morning after sourdough pancakes at the RV park's breakfast room, we inquired in the office where we might get the appropriate parts needed to fix our pipe. Although we'd seen plenty of gas stations, garages, and windshield-repair places on the way in, none of them had what we needed. There was no RV supply place in town. Joyce, our hostess, made a few calls for us, but no one had what we needed. Thanking her, we headed into Tok on our bikes to see what we could cobble together.

The unexpected interruption made clear something that had been percolating inside us. One of the changes I noticed in both of us was a relative increase in patience. That's not to say that we had enjoyed waiting on line for the ferry back in Dawson, but our plumbing problem seemed an adventure rather than a pain in the ass. We didn't get crazed about having one day in our precious vacation "ruined." It wasn't a problem to stay another night, since we didn't have a slew of other reservations to juggle. Fixing the pipe became a challenge and an opportunity. This was a very strange new attitude indeed. Besides, it gave Sandy the opportunity to apply some of the information he'd picked up from all those years of watching *This Old House.*

While a busted water pipe wasn't something either of us would have chosen as an amusement, it gave us a good excuse to get to know Tok a bit. Unlike towns in New England, the South, and the Southwest, this one had no center or plaza. Just east of a strip of gas stations, stores, and services was the junction of the road we'd come in on from Dawson and the Alaska Highway from Whitehorse. Just west of the new information center, the Alaska Highway continued north to Fairbanks, and the Glenn Highway took off in a southwesterly direction for Anchorage. Shamrock Hardware was somewhere in between. Bob, the non-Irish proprietor from New Hampshire, absorbed the details of our problem. He reminded us of Bob Vila, complete with Yankee accent. He asked many questions about the size of the pipe, the opening it went through, the way it was currently sealed, and what tools we had with us. It was clear he enjoyed this sort of puzzle, a sort of mechanical equivalent of nail soup. We walked the aisles of the store together, looking for items that might be conjoined to create a new pipe and leakproof fitting. The PVC we found was either too large or small, but we thought we could engineer a good seal inside a looser opening. The exact joint we needed wasn't there either, but we substituted. We also snagged a small saw with which we planned to create a larger opening for it, so it wouldn't have to rest on unfinished lumber anymore. Bob sent us off and wished us good luck. We pedaled back to camp and got to work.

Sawing the wood was awkward but simple. Since I was the smaller of the two of us, I won this assignment. I couldn't get good purchase, wedged into the basement lying on my side, or much swing to my upward stroke, but I grated away at the opening. Once it was big enough, Sandy got to work removing the old pipe and fitting the new one. Meanwhile I worked on blow-drying the carpet. Six years earlier, when we'd bought our first house, Sandy had warned me that every plumbing job he'd ever attempted had to be done twice: the first time and the right time. As I turned on the hose to test the fix, I kept my fingers crossed that he would defy his own prediction. When I heard "Stop!" I knew it was not to be. Back to town for a second consult with Bob.

First, however, we were introduced to a fine Alaskan tradition: the salmon bake. Combining the best of a barbecue and a clambake, the concept at the Gateway restaurant was simple. We placed our order for freshly grilled salmon, halibut, or ribs with Cleta, who passed it on to Dave, her husband and the chef. Meanwhile we were directed to help ourselves to soup— salmon chowder. Next stop was a salad bar. Since only cold crops grow easily this far north, there were mounds of cole slaw. Other salads, as well as sourdough rolls, iced tea, and lemonade, were plentiful. Since it was vaguely sunny, we opted for an outside picnic table. When Dave called out, "Marilyn and Sandy from New York," we fetched our food and were invited to scoop up a ladle of Alaskan baked beans. As we sat facing the road and the sun, other diners came and went, nodding hello and peering at our selections. I felt as if I were eating salmon for the first time. A slightly sweet, light glaze on the fish made it crispy on the outside while keeping it moist within. Juice dribbled down toward Sandy's wrists as he hoisted hefty beef ribs. We licked our fingers and traded plates. The ribs were excellent: beefy and not too slathered in sauce. We ate as much as we could and bundled up the rest for another time. I thought about all the pretentious, expensive meals I'd had and shook my head at their inadequacies. This was surely Northern Nirvana.

Thus fortified, we headed back to the Shamrock. A different size pipe, other clamps, some Space Age glue, another "good luck" from Bob, and we got back on our bikes. On the way we noticed a bakery and couldn't resist picking up a few sourdough rolls to go with our leftovers, and a pair of bearclaws— doughnuts by any other name—for breakfast. Back at the ranch Sandy got into position to do the plumbing deed. After a lot of cursing, screwing, and drilling, it was time to test. I opened the water flow gradually, waiting for the shout to stop. It didn't come. Our leak was history, and we were victorious. We had jerry-rigged a home improvement that Tim Allen would have been proud of.

Even though we had spent an extra day in Tok doing unexpected chores rather than hiking or moving on, it felt as if we'd achieved something miraculous—a survival test of sorts. The pipe no longer dripped, the carpet was dry, and we were as giddy about our success as if we'd just struck gold in Alaska.

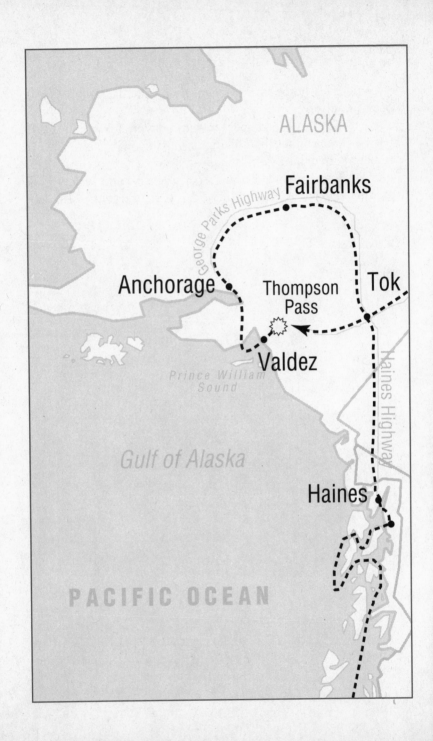

10

Baked Alaska

We had been in Alaska only two days, but already we felt an enormous freedom. Driven by silliness, we called for a calendar check—something we did regularly at home to make sure we hadn't double-booked ourselves for dinners or committed the other one to attending an event they couldn't make because of a conflict. Opening our respective day books, we noticed just three appointments for the coming five weeks: a ferry reservation from Valdez to Seward on the fifth; a date at the airport in Anchorage on the tenth to pick up my dad; another ferry reservation in Haines at the end of August. We tossed our calendars into the deep recesses of our closet and toasted our brilliant getaway with diet Cokes. We'd already been on the road four weeks, longer than any previous vacation, including our honeymoon, and it felt as if something fresh were just beginning.

Everywhere we looked, we seemed to be on an unfamiliar planet. The mountains were bigger than those we were used to, even bigger than the Rockies. They were craggier, sharper, younger than those old gently rounded mounds of the East. Even in July many were snow-capped. The streams were either crystal clear and packed with spawning fish, or else they were lifeless and the opaque emerald green of glacial runoff. We slowed down as moose strolled across the highway. Ice-blue glacier fingers oozed down mountains toward us in slow motion. There was no poison ivy here, so I would not be spending this summer in itch hell, as I often had. Snakes, apparently, could not survive the climate either. What a shame. Even the feared and dreaded giant mosquitoes failed to appear.

As we toodled south on the Glenn Highway, cocky from our recent home-repair success, we decided to push the envelope a little more. We took the Edgerton Cut-off toward McCarthy and the defunct Kennicott Copper Mines. All around us, deep forests encroached more upon the road with each mile. Occasionally a log home would appear, the yard often cluttered with snow machines, pickup trucks under repair, spare airplane tires or pontoons, and other paraphernalia of bush survival. While most places were inhabited, one or two were abandoned and covered with graffiti fiercely decrying the last owner's unjust run-ins with the authorities. It became clear to us that the tools we used to evaluate unfamiliar terrain—how manicured the lawns were, the tidiness of the driveways—were not useful in a land where staying alive takes priority over lifestyle.

It was exciting to be in this more remote area, and we appreciated the flexibility of being in an RV. Wherever we were, we were home. As we looked for a place to spend the night, we read about Liberty Falls Recreational Area in our guidebook: "large RV's and trailers check road before driving in; 5 sites, no water; no camping fee. Berry picking, watch for bears." It sounded perfect. We pulled off near the tiny turn-off, and I went to scout the situation. Up a hill, beyond a bridge rated for eight tons (we were seven and a half), I saw a picture-postcard campsite. It was next to a stream with a waterfall. I thought we could squeeze into it. I went back and told Sandy to come ahead. Carefully driving the twisting dirt road, he was able to maneuver the Sue into position facing the waterfall. We pulled out our eighteen-foot awning, lawn chairs, and drinks and made ourselves at home. We were exuberant at being on our own, unplugged and unhooked, yet fully prepared to cook up a wonderful meal and stare at the stars with the aid of a telescope and a guidebook. If only we could have stayed up late enough to catch the sunset sometime after midnight.

Years earlier I had learned to cook out of necessity when my mother died. I was fifteen, and my father had arranged to have grandmotherly Mrs. Weinstock come in to make supper for us. Following several overboiled, underseasoned dinners, I volunteered to take over. Filling up the empty after-school apartment with the noise of egg beaters clanging against bowls and the smell of onions browning in butter made me a little less lonesome. Even then I cared enough about a good meal not to mind taking the time to learn how to make one. How hard could it be? I thought.

Dad—Pop, as I sometimes called him—bought me *The New York Times International Cookbook* for encouragement. Lester and Freddy, our friendly neighborhood butchers, always jotted instructions on my package of meat. I was the only kid I knew who came home from school to watch Julia Child on public television. She deserves credit for taking the fear out of cooking for me. So what if she dropped that big slippery fish on the floor? She would just pick it up, wash it off, and keep going. Nothing ever intimidated Julia, as I referred to her after a while. Pop loved her veal scallopini. Fridays we usually ate out (Italian), and mostly we were invited for dinner at some friend's house on Saturdays. I'd hang out in the kitchen with the hostess and watch her work. I mastered veal with mushrooms and wine, lamb chops, and London broil. What eluded me, however, was mushroom gravy for the latter. I used canned broth or bouillon cubes, onions and mushrooms, following the recipes I found.

The results were lumpy and bland. The curse of Mrs. W, perhaps? I cajoled a kid in the neighborhood to be my taster. (His parents had taken to dining fashionably late, or perhaps they merely extended the cocktail hour to two or three, so this growing lad was always hungry and ate anything.) He was kind and encouraged my efforts, but we both knew I had met my culinary Waterloo. Eventually Julia clued me in to the fact that you really need an actual roast or bones from which to make good gravy. For the time being, this was beyond me. Sadder but wiser, I moved on to new challenges. My burgeoning cooking expertise attracted kids to hang out at our house: who else offered up trays of canapés and homemade eggnog for after-school snacks? The lucky ones were invited to stay for suppers of shrimp scampi or Wiener schnitzel—very avant-garde home cooking in those days, but then again I was learning from an *international* cookbook and Julia, the French chef. It was years before I would master ordinary macaroni and cheese. I continued cooking during college, when the house favorites, in tune with the times, became earthy foods like banana bread.

Once I began working (I even edited cookbooks for a while), I ran out of gas for cooking. When Sandy married me twenty-something years later, I was a New York career woman. He had become accustomed to dining out and had a strict "no used food" (leftovers) policy. It worked out perfectly, since what I made best for dinner on weekdays was reservations. I could also handle take-out or ordering in. Beyond that, I had the time and inclination to prepare food for friends and family only on weekends. Happily, it became a team effort with Sandy as grill man, baker, and sometime salad chef. We enjoyed preparing feasts together, but I could no sooner have cooked every night than I could have walked naked through Times Square. I simply didn't have it in me.

On the road all that changed. First, the expense of eating in restaurants was annoying. Then it was fun stopping at a local market to pick up supplies along with a sense of the town.

Finally, although breakfast and lunch were usually on the run, we both enjoyed preparing a leisurely supper together. We preferred a cookout when the weather was fine and saved a few "indoor" recipes for other times. That night we grilled chicken by the falls and had that fine dessert of international renown, s'mores.

* * *

The next day we drove a short way down the McCarthy Road, then squeezed through a cut between two rocks so narrow, I had to get out a run ahead to see if we could make it. We could, just barely, but we were flummoxed a little bit farther on, where the dirt road disintegrated to one that could accommodate only small four-wheel-drive vehicles. The land around us looked as dried up as the riverbed we'd crossed. Native fish wheels hung over a trickle of water. I hoped for their sake it would rain soon. We banged a U-y (it's not easy to make a U-turn in a 29′ 10″ vehicle) and aimed south.

The weather turned mean, looking suspiciously as if it might snow as we approached Thompson Pass, the snowiest place in Alaska. A sign told us the annual record was a monumental 974.5 inches, just over 81 feet. Along the road upside-down L's towered above us, guides indicating to snowplow drivers where to plow when there were twenty feet or better of snow. The fog, mist, and wind convinced us to pull into a site at Blueberry Lake Campground, which we read would have a great view when the storm subsided. Optimistically, we put on full Gore-Tex gear and went for a hike. It was nasty out. Finding the eponymous lake, we headed over toward a rocky meadow. Little was blooming, and we couldn't find any blueberries. Every now and then a break in the clouds would offer a tantalizing peek at the alpine-like mountain vista, then hide it again. The cold was seeping through my gear. A few other RVs and tents dotted the scene, but most people were indoors. We ran into a few dog walkers, but we seemed to be the only ones who were outside of our own volition. The weather failed to improve. We opted for bunk games. When I was a kid in camp and we had foul weather, counselors would struggle to think up games and contests to keep us amused. Somehow Sandy and I didn't have that problem. It was also a good way to keep warm.

Later on we found a local public radio station that had some good talk and music. We wrote e-mail, saving it for the day when we could actually send it, and read our books. Sandy had raced through *Wilderness Seasons,* the memoir he'd bought in Whitehorse, and suggested I have a go at it. It was ironic that I'd originally gotten into publishing because I loved books yet as the years went on had had less and less time to read what I wanted. There was always a stack of proposals to read and manuscripts to edit.

Having the opportunity to read the same book Sandy had and discuss it, like real people, was fabulous. First, however, I had to finish *E.* The RV was cozy. As all the windows fogged up and the mist grew thicker, we couldn't tell where inside and outside met. Although the propane heater did an admirable job, the dampness was getting to me. I decided it was time to see what the oven could do. We had never used it, and it took me some time to figure out how to light the thing, but eventually it warmed up. I checked our cookbooks. We had brought along three. Two were well-used favorites: *Master Recipes* by Stephen Schmidt, a wonderful cook's bible, and *Relax, It's Only Dinner* by Cheryl Merser, a very clever cook who could make a feast out of an empty pantry. The last was a small gift-type book we'd published but I'd never used, called *Cupcakes* by Cerri Hada. Somehow I'd thought to bring this along, as well as a muffin tin, envisioning just this kind of day. Checking the recipe list against our supplies, I chose orange nut muffins. It wasn't baked Alaska, but they were tasty, perfumed the air with orange and vanilla, and warmed both the RV and us. Dinner that night was one of our foul-weather contingencies, Sandy's favorite pasta: a hearty mélange of garlic, onion, crumbled hot sausage, tomato, and cream over rigatoni.

In the morning the weather cleared, and after a breakfast of homemade muffins, we went on to Valdez (pronounced *Valdeez*). As we approached, the lush scenery continued to surprise us. Alternating between verdant narrow canyons lined with waterfalls and expansive views of the snowy Chugach, Wrangell, and St. Elias ranges, the Great Land was great indeed.

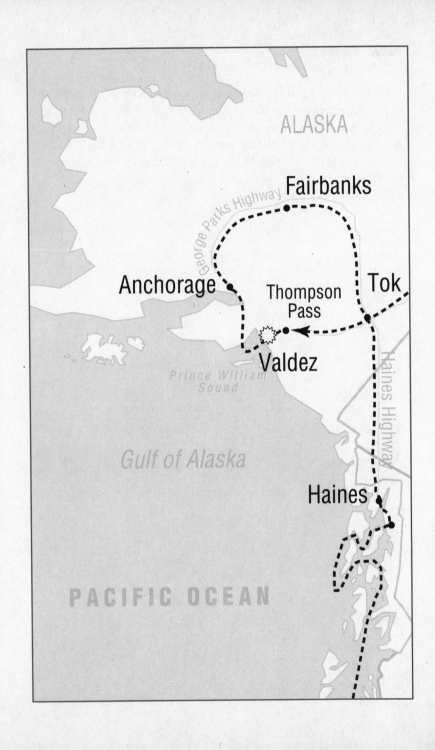

11

It's a Man Thing

By the time we got to Valdez, we were ready for a break from driving. We planted ourselves at the water's edge, facing the expansive natural beauty of the snowy fjord and the geometric man-made grandeur of the pipeline terminus. The view encapsulated the weird juxtaposition that is Alaska. Fifteen feet from our window, a sea otter lolled on his back as he used a rock to crack open some shellfish for lunch. Across the harbor several supertankers lined up to suckle crude oil. It was a picture postcard of man and nature coexisting in Eden. When it worked. When it didn't, as happened early one morning in March 1989, when the Exxon *Valdez* ran aground on Bligh Reef in Prince William Sound just outside this harbor, it was a disaster.

After more than five thousand miles of driving, we were able to relax for a few days. We unhitched our bikes and went off to find the area's trails. We pedaled toward the pipeline terminus but didn't quite make it. Instead we watched as tourists and locals lined up in the shallows at the top of the harbor to fish. RVs would park here for weeks, we were told, at this precious rich spot. It was a deceptive and odd place to catch the salmon that were struggling to find their birthplace in order to spawn: we were downstream from a fish hatchery. Amazing how a fish could find its way "home," even if it was essentially a test tube.

After exploring all day, we cruised by the visitor information center. As a New Yorker, it had taken some getting used to, but by now I knew we could leave our bikes without necessarily attaching them to a post with a kryptonite lock. It gave me a tiny knot of discomfort, but I could handle it. (I couldn't, however, leave the Sue unlocked. I wasn't that mellow and probably never would be.) At the VC we picked up some brochures and caught a flick about the 1964 Good Friday earthquake. The devastation here had been complete. A 9.2 on the Richter scale, this quake had leveled the old town of Valdez, forcing the creation of the new town site, where we now were, four miles west of the original. The quake had dropped the ritzy residential area of Anchorage into the sea. Earthquake Park was developed in its wake. Yet another example of life's impermanence, I thought. Perhaps I was musing to myself about this as I left the visitors' center. Or maybe my legs were wobbly from the day of riding. But somehow, as I flung my left leg over the bike to leave, I heaved a bit too enthusiastically and went completely over the top onto my left side, jamming the bike against my shinbone. People came running out to see if "the lady" (was someone else hurt too?) was okay, as Sandy untangled me from myself. "Fine," I muttered as I hobbled to a bench. I gently pressed my bone and knew it wasn't broken, but man, it was killing me. As Sandy ran off to the drugstore to get a chemical ice pack, I laughed to myself and thought I was the only person I knew who could have a bicycle accident standing still.

Riding a bike is probably an exciting thing to learn when you're, say, four or five. But when you grow up in Manhattan and you have overprotective parents, the true pleasures of pedaling may not be yours until you're, say, forty-five. Take me, for example. My parents' refusal to buy me a bike led directly to my clamoring to ride one and badgering a summer camp counselor to give me a lesson or two. Being averagely agile, it shouldn't have been a problem to maneuver on, if not master, a bike the way my twelve-year-old cohorts did. Practicing on my own one afternoon, however, I went down a short gravelly hill that veered off toward the left. Unfortunately, I veered off to the right, resulting in severe lacerations plus the sickening sensation that my parents had been right. Bikes were not for me. I could have all the books, Bach, and ballet I wanted, but bikes were for kids in Iowa, wherever that was.

Years passed. Plenty of other things surfaced to cause *agita* between me and my parents—sex, drugs, rock 'n' roll. Riding a bike seemed to be, if ever I thought about it, just another child-hood thing that was over, even if it had never really begun. So the earth spun around another decade or so, and I found myself at a beach house on Nantucket that I had rented with my cousin, Claire, her two kids, and seventeen of our best friends. Nantucket is a lovely island, thirty miles or so off Cape Cod, very beachy and very preppy, and to some extent it still has the veneer of being not overly developed. One way this quaintness is encouraged is by the renting of bikes. Numerous paths around the island service those who like to think they've found a way back to a simpler time.

It wasn't so simple for me. There were still clumps of scar tissue here and there on my body to prove it. Many of our housemates brought their own bikes and chatted over dinner about touring the next day. When the time came to saddle up, I tried hiding in the bathroom, hoping they would leave without me. No luck. Barry, a dear friend of mine yet somehow a natural jock (I don't exaggerate—he ran marathons), and a few of the others decided to ride to the far end of the island. I disappeared. Barry came looking for me. He banged on the bathroom door. "Come on, let's go." I was mute. Mature too. "I know you're in there." I hated him at that minute. "It'll be fun. You'll see. It's a flat, easy ride." I hated him and my parents for getting me into this humiliating scene. He banged some more. I could hear the shuffling of several dozen feet. Someone else knocked, needing to use the john. I vacated my sanctuary with great reluctance.

On a rented bike that terrified me and killed my butt, I puffed along. Far behind the others, I ranted to myself about the not-flatness of the island. The little bit of traffic we had to deal with overwhelmed me into near paralysis. I thought my head would explode from the heat, my lungs from the lack of air. I didn't sweat—I turned red. The scenery was gorgeous, and I loved going down the not-hills. On the way back we stopped for sodas. I had figured out how the gears worked. (The last time I had tried this, there were no gears.) By the time the group arrived back at the house, I hated Barry less. In time I would pedal parts of the New York marathon route with him as he trained. By then I had bought my own bike, with a seat that didn't hurt quite so much, and had learned to conquer traffic my own way. I insisted we go out at six on Sunday mornings. In the following years Sandy and I had pedaled many miles together.

Now Sandy returned from the drugstore and applied the ice pack to my shin. The pain seemed to localize, and I could see a purplish bruise but nothing more. Luckily we had only a mile or so to ride back to camp. Once there I rested some more. As the pain gave way to hunger, I knew I was okay. Someone recommended the Totem Inn for dinner. I managed to pedal there without too much trouble. Good thing too. Otherwise we never would have discovered the most perfect halibut and chips on earth. I had first eaten halibut in my college dorm cafeteria. It looked like a perfect white rectangle and tasted exactly like lukewarm, reconstituted, dried Styrofoam. I'd avoided it ever since. Sandy's impressions were similar, and we only ordered it now because the waitress was so enthused about it. The platter placed in front of us had mounds of batter-dipped, deep-fried, moist fresh fish and piles of fries. A little hot sauce, lemon, and ketchup, and we were in Alaskan heaven.

It was a pleasant change to be in one place for a few days. Somehow having a day of lousy weather didn't seem so cruel, and it gave us a chance to take care of two important things: e-mail and laundry. Despite all of our efforts to set up a mobile office, we were often foiled by lack of cellular service or of reciprocity of service with our carrier. This was especially true in Canada. Back in the States we'd hoped for better service, and at the Sea Otter RV Park we really lucked out. This was the only place we stayed that was equipped with individual offices. Each space (larger than a booth, smaller than a room) had two stools, a counter where you could write or put a computer, and a phone/phone line that accepted local, credit card, or 800-number calls. We were in business at last. Once or twice a day while we were there, we'd set up shop to pick up or send mail. Sandy, the numbers guy who swore he couldn't write, had started keeping a journal that he originally sent to a short list of friends.

Word got around, and we received requests from others who wanted to be added to the distribution. Our address list grew. We began to correspond with people who had been mere acquaintances when we left home but became good friends as the miles went by. We shared our adventures with them, and they told us what was going on in their lives and in the business. It was so exciting to get news from home. There was even e-gossip: people changing jobs, having babies, getting married. We were thrilled to be in touch from our "office."

The other bit of necessity was laundry. We'd brought plenty of clothes, but underwear was running low. Since there was a large Laundromat on the premises and I was still limping a little and thought better of hiking, I volunteered to do the wash. Sandy offered to help, but I said I just needed a hand getting the stuff to the laundry room and back. There were at least a dozen each, washers and dryers, all with a great view. For some reason, something got something started in me. Although Valdez looks like Switzerland (peaky snow-patched mountains surrounding deep blue water), it brought out the Nashville in me. I'll let you have it one time. Here goes. (The words fit into just about any country tune of your choice.)

It's a Man Thing

It was a cloudy Wednesday morning and I had some time to kill,
So I thought I'd do my laundry in the town of oil spill.
My hubby is a gent and he agreed to help me out—
He heaved the clothes, the Tide, the Bounce, even brought the
  Shout.

The Laundromat, the Laundromat, it's the place to be—
You can find out the weather, the road news, and have tea.
The Laundromat, the Laundromat, it's toasty here and dry;
Outside the wind is howling though it's the middle of July.

There's some kind of satisfaction, though not the kind Mick
  meant,
When your clothes are done tumblin', your quarters have been
  spent,
To fold the shirts and towels, forming towering piles
And the hubby comes to get you and offers up a smile.

The Laundromat, etc.

"But honey, where's the laundry bag? I left it on the door."
"I swear I didn't see it, wasn't there anymore."
Now I get a mite impatient, start to twist my wedding ring,
When the lady to my right says, "Honey, it's a man thing."

The Laundromat, etc.

"Honey, have you noticed that your husband or your man
Will stand at the refrigerator lost as a lamb,
Whining 'Where'd you put the butter? where'd you put the jam?'
But he can spot good knockers a mile away, goddamn."

The Laundromat, etc.

How can you believe a man when he says he likes your looks,
When he can't see the laundry bag that's hanging on the hook?
When he's got to walk right through it in order to get out?
Then that gal reminds me, "Honey, it's a man thing," she
    shouts.

The Laundromat, etc.

Since quitting my job, I'd been concentrating on the idea of
change. A lot of people say you never know when, where, or
how that next career is going to strike. Now that I'd gotten over
writing hit country tunes, I could move on to something else.
And Trisha Yearwood could relax too. In the meantime my husband looked mighty good to me. I would learn something remarkable about him on this trip. Even if he couldn't see the
laundry bag in front of his nose, he could spot wildlife (one
word, the furry kind) a half-mile away. Perhaps the hunter instinct is for real. It's a man thing.

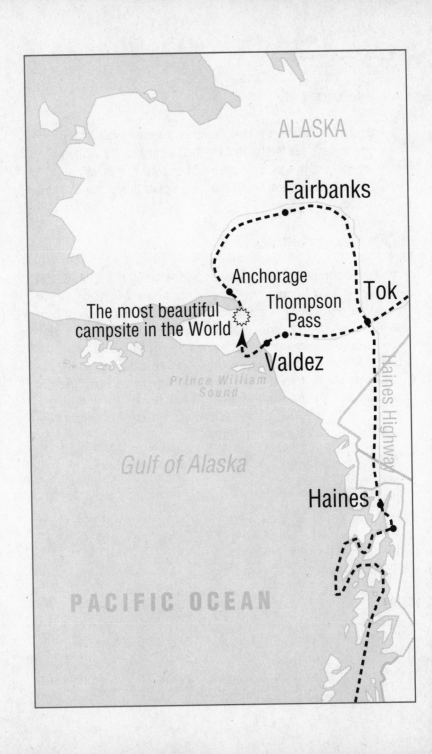

12

Salmon 101

*I*always thought of lox first. Salmon was an afterthought. Growing up in New York, bagels and lox took precedence over, beyond, and to the exclusion of actually fishing for salmon. At our campground in Valdez, I watched in awe as people came home with strings of freshly caught salmon, popped them into their portable smokers, and turned them into something that goes for twenty dollars a pound in Manhattan. Even though the exact process may be different, making lox was quite a new concept for me.

Fishing is a megasport in Alaska. We had seen people standing shoulder to shoulder, tossing out lines. They were engaged in what we later found out was called combat fishing. It seemed that everyone in the state except us, and maybe every fisherperson on the planet, knew the salmon were running. We asked someone what the story was. The reply was partially in English. "The reds are running, but you gotta use flies. The silvers haven't started yet. Kings are off limits in the Russian, but you could go for them with spinners in the Kenai. Pinks are on even years only. Dogs is dogs. If you can't find a good place here, go downriver and play catch and release with the rainbow. Or try for Dollies with a spinner, winged bobber, or small weighted spoon." And all my life I'd thought salmon came two ways: poached or smoked. Turned out there were five kinds of salmon in Alaskan waters, and each had at least one other name: king (Chinook), sockeye (red), silver (coho), pink (humpback), and chum (dog). Each could be caught with different lines, at different times in varying locations. All would eventually be canned, most were smoked, and some were shipped out frozen. The local preference was clearly for king steaks. They were the tastiest fish, in my opinion, because they were flush with fat, often three times as much as chum. The largest reported king weighed in at 126 pounds. This time of year there were salmon derbies everywhere, and the purse could run into thousands of dollars.

*   *   *

Another of the many things that continued to surprise us about Alaska was the roads. The state is over half a million square miles, twice the size of Texas, yet there are fewer than three thousand miles of mapped roads. There is a cluster of roads in south-central, of which about half promise to be paved. Only one road runs north-south through the central portion, a thousand miles from Prudhoe Bay to Seward. Only half of that is paved. I transposed that in my mind to the East Coast. The equivalent would be a smooth ride from Columbia, South Carolina, to Washington, D.C., then dirt roads to Augusta, Maine. Amazing. The rest of the state is as reachable as it has always been—by river in summer, by dogsled team in winter. And there are planes. Almost everyone seemed to have a little something out in the yard. Most of the planes were single-engine privately owned, though many were for hire for "flightseeing." It seemed wild to us that Juneau, the capital, couldn't be reached overland, only by sea or air. So many places are inaccessible by road that the state has created a very extensive Marine Highway

System. Eight ships traverse 3,500 miles of the state's 47,000-mile coastline. In order to avoid backtracking and continue on new paths, we'd booked passage on the ferry from Valdez to Seward, a twelve-hour trip. We wondered how they would accommodate the RV, but when we saw the ship, we realized immediately how foolish we'd been. These boats are the lifeline for many communities. Food, fuel, and the trucks they came in were transported this way every day. One thirty-foot RV was more or less a drop in the old bucket for these ships. Another thing we hadn't anticipated was having a tour guide onboard: a park ranger and her good pal, Smokey the Bear. The ranger pointed out Columbia Glacier, blue with light trapped in hundreds of feet of ice. She called our attention to whales, dolphins, common murres (a penguin look-alike), seals, otters, and puffins. Puffins, small black and white birds with overlarge, cartoonish orange bills, are goofy-looking. If they didn't exist, Disney would have invented them. In the meantime the poor things are widely pictured throughout Alaska in the middle of the international "no" symbol as a sign not to smoke. No puffin. Cute. This is the only thing about Alaska that qualifies as "cute." This is the last frontier, the Great Land. It's a rugged place: you can die of exposure here in August. No puffin? It must have been thought up by someone from out of state, we decided. Smokey posed for pictures with the kids. And Sandy.

While we cruised along, we realized we had to adjust our habits for my dad's upcoming visit. As game as he was to come out, our totally winging-it lifestyle was not quite suitable for an eighty-year-old gent from the old country. I doubt he'd ever been on a vacation without making reservations. We thought about what he might like to do, took note of things we could do together, and knowing how much he loved to eat out, read up on restaurants we might try. We also wondered how his two-week visit would affect us. Could our boat float with fifty percent more personnel?

*   *   *

We explored the Kenai Peninsula, the scenic area that juts into the Gulf of Alaska just below Anchorage. We hiked when the mood moved us, camped when we got tired, and drove on when we wanted to see something new. Towns, for the most part, were beside the point here, we concluded. They were service hubs, only somewhat expanded from the old days, which meant you could now rent a video when you picked up some supplies. These days there were plenty of auto and windshield repair places along with the dry goods and grocery stores. In case we got a sudden urge to go fishing, many places—drugstores to gas stations—stocked fishing gear. I saw more varieties of lures than I'd ever imagined existed. My favorite was the Pixie—a gaudy pink and silver thing designed to attract salmon. What did they use for cream cheese? I wondered.

I needn't have. There was any kind of cheese, from cream to cheddar, blue, Brie, and more, in Alaska. Ripe pineapples, avocados, and mangoes seemed easier to find here than on Broadway. Life, and the people living it out here, was far more sophisticated than I could ever have imagined from my catbird seat in Rockefeller Center. We had expected to be "roughing" it, but food tastes were hardly primitive. Olive oils, balsamic and raspberry vinegars, all kinds of mustards and barbecue sauces lined the shelves. Then came enormous international sections with complete lines of Thai, Chinese, and Indian goodies. We felt pretty stupid having toted all those condiments up from New York.

In the meat department we found anything we wanted, except yellow chickens. We'd noticed early on, beginning in the plains, that the chickens were white. They looked pale and sickly to us, so we avoided buying them. Eventually as the desire for grilled chicken nearly overwhelmed us, we asked a butcher what the story was. Evidently, we were naive victims of geography: in some places, chicken feed contains more corn giving the birds' skin a robust glow. Over the years we had become as accustomed to these blond birds as, say, to orange cheddar. Realizing our error, we were surprised to find the white birds tasted "regular" in every way. I guess they would need a little extra sunblock at the beach, but on the grill they were every bit as tasty as their brethren back home.

Bakeries offered all kinds of tasty temptations, from sour-dough breads to enormous cinnamon buns. Then there was all the fresh fish, shrimp, and crab that came in daily. It was clear we could forget about subsisting on macaroni and cheese.

*   *   *

Our education in fish continued one afternoon as we strolled down a quiet dirt road. We came to a little bridge. All around, fishermen were casting and reeling in, casting and reeling in Dollies—Dolly Varden, a fifteen-to-twenty-inch fish that was abundant in the area. It was a calm spot, not a combat zone, surrounded by piney woods, men, women, and children. It was an almost idyllic scene of summer. Then we noticed The Man. As if this were an old Western movie, people started edging away from this guy. We sensed tension in the air. He went over to question one of the fishermen, who showed him his license. The lawman nodded, then looked around. People had vanished, it seemed, into the forest. The crowd had definitely thinned out. What was going on here? we wondered. It was explained to us later that long before Seward bought the place, fishing had been a way of life and livelihood in Alaska. As a natural resource, fish were closely watched. Fishing was strictly regulated and moni-tored as to time, place, and what was used to catch the fish. Some individuals clearly did not want to be told what to do. We'd never before seen a fish and game warden who wore a bulletproof vest and carried extra rounds for his nine-millimeter. The gun might have been bear protection, but somehow I doubted that the vest was. We watched the fishing for a while. Maybe we'd have to give in and try it before we left. Our first order of business just then was to find a place to spend the night.

On the shores of Kenai Lake we found "the best campsite in Alaska," according to the two disappointed silver-haired couples who arrived from Anchorage just after we had settled in. They came down to camp at this exact spot at least once a year. Since sites were spoken for on a first-come-first-served basis, they were a little hangdog about the fact that we'd gotten there first. Even after forty years of living in Alaska, they said, they still couldn't get over the beauty of it. We promised we'd give them first crack at our location when we were ready to leave, but we weren't about to vacate for anyone or anything. For seven dollars a night, we camped directly on the emerald-green glacier-fed Kenai Lake with a terrific view of the mountains. In our woodsy space was a picnic table, a fire ring, and a path leading to the beach. We brought our new neighbors some firewood as a sort of peace offering or consolation prize. They gladly accepted, and we chatted for a while as the two men took turns chopping some of our logs into fine kindling. It occurred to me that I'd rarely seen such fit senior citizens. They told us they'd come to fish and would be off early in the morning.

We were beginning to understand the passion people felt about fishing, though we were not yet moved to do it ourselves. Instead, we set off on our bikes—a much more intimate way to see the world than from the Sue. Pedaling along the dirt road, we noticed a smaller road leading off this one that we'd missed from the altitude of the RV. We followed it to find a small grassy strip. There was no terminal, no building or equipment of any kind. Not even a windsock. Just a relatively flat piece of land with eight or ten small planes parked at one end. We snooped around a bit, peeking into the planes. One five-seater was littered with the everyday detritus of suburbia: a football helmet, several coloring books, a couple of plastic water bottles, and sweaters. The station wagon of the North. We hung around awhile, hoping to get someone to take us up. As we waited, a plane landed, letting off several passengers who were guests at a nearby lodge. The pilot chatted with us a bit but said he had just about enough fuel to get him back to Seward and couldn't take us. We waved as he drove off along the grass and popped into the sky. Just as we were about to give up loitering, someone pulled up in a car. A tall slim gentleman with salt and pepper hair peeking out from the edges of a baseball cap came over toward us. We introduced ourselves. We asked Lyman Nichols if he had a plane here that he'd be able to give us a tour in. The good news was he had a plane; the bad news was it had only one passenger seat. He was free-lancing for fish and game and had to go up and count sheep. A dream job? We watched Lyman and his little plane bounce down the field, bobbing as it lifted across the lake toward the mountains.

*   *   *

The next day we lounged in our lawn chairs by the lake. I'd learned to combat the pervasive chilliness with ski pants, turtle-necks, and warm boots, refusing to be forced in out of the cold. It drizzled often, and we were quite content to be out and about in Gore-Tex gear. Although it wasn't the kind of shorts and T-shirt, baking-in-the-hot-sun summer weather we were used to, we accommodated easily and gladly for the chance to take in the scenery. I became deeply engrossed in *Wilderness Seasons,* the book Sandy had just finished reading. It was the story of a young Vancouver couple who spent fourteen months in the Brit-ish Columbia outback. Wayback. They had chosen their spot because it was remote and on a lake. They had been airlifted in with a load of supplies. They built their own cabin, felling and stripping every log by hand. When their second airlifted load of supplies failed to appear, they learned to track, kill, and butcher their first moose. Their communication problem was even worse than ours: Their radio failed to work entirely. In winter they often woke up to temperatures below freezing inside. Somehow we both loved reading this story and related to it as a distant, far braver cousin of our own trip. Grilling up a skirt steak mari-nated in garlic, chili paste, and soy sauce, I wondered if this would be good on moose. That night as I took a nice hot shower and blow-dried my hair, I realized, with something of a shock, that living in the Transue, with propane heat, a roof that didn't leak, a microwave oven, and a refrigerator freezer, was the height of luxury. What a difference in our perspective one month had made.

As I was getting dressed the next morning, a car drove by our site very slowly. Since we knew lots of other sites were available, this seemed odd and somehow threatening. Our city antennae went up. "Intruder. Intruder. Intruder," a little electronic voice in my head said. At least it was daylight, I thought. Then again, it was light around here about twenty hours a day. Crime must go way down here in summer, I hoped. I scrambled to get my layers on. Sandy went out to investigate. I wondered whether I would be able to load the rifle if I had to. Unlikely. Maybe it was someone else who wanted this campsite. No way. We'd promised it to the people across the street. I speed-laced my boots and went out. There was Sandy having a chat with Lyman, the pilot from the day before. It seems he felt so badly about not being able to give us a ride in his plane, he came back to ask us over to have coffee and meet his wife. I felt just a little like a giant jerk at that instant.

Lyman and Gladys Nichols, originally from Louisiana and New York respectively, met through the mail thirteen years ago. He was living in Alaska, was divorced, and had raised his son Robert and daughter Jody. A friend suggested he might want to correspond with a woman he knew back east. Gladys, divorced and the mother of a ten-year-old girl, was working and living in Pennsylvania. The correspondence went on for eighteen months, at which point they agreed on a visit. Gladys would fly up to Alaska, and if she and Lyman hit it off in person as well as they had in writing, she would stay. It was a lock. Gladys and her daughter, Kim, moved to Cooper Landing, population 386. The wedding took place in Seward. As all the kids in small towns in Alaska did, Kim boarded with a family during the week (between Soldotna and Kenai, forty-six miles away) for junior and senior high. She came home on weekends. After attending college up in Fairbanks, she settled there with her husband. Her parents couldn't understand why they wanted to live in such a cold place.

Gladys and Lyman had built the home we visited, a lovely retreat on the river. Jewellike soldiers, including purple fireweed jelly and other items from the garden put up by Gladys, stood guarding the mud-room entrance. They'd made most everything in the house themselves, including the kitchen cabinets. Gladys, a handsome woman with an elegant figure, even in jeans, laughed when she told us of a telephone surveyer who had once asked her in which supermarket she bought her meat. She explained that they killed a caribou every year, a moose every other. Lyman teased her gently about the first moose she'd bagged, years ago. Got a good one and got him clean, didn't take a lot of shooting. Only trouble was they were a mile and a half from the road. Did we have any idea what it was like for two average-size people to lug a dead moose that far? It was difficult for us to picture. They smiled sweetly at each other. Their meat freezer, they explained, was right outside. It was plugged in only during the summer, of course, not in the winter. When they wanted salmon, they went out back and caught one. They grew what they could in this climate, though Gladys was giving herself and the garden this year off. In spring they planned to take a trip "outside" to visit Jody and her five children in California. Of course they'd fly their own plane. We had coffee and tea and chatted in the cozy kitchen. Outside, as we left, a squirrel that had been trained to run up the outside of their pants leg to search and seize the peanut hidden in a pocket there for him, put in an appearance. As Lyman drove us back to our campsite, I thought maybe this was what Thoreau had had in mind. And all our friends who had tittered and nattered about our "relationship risks" on taking this trip ought to have coffee at the Nichols's sometime.

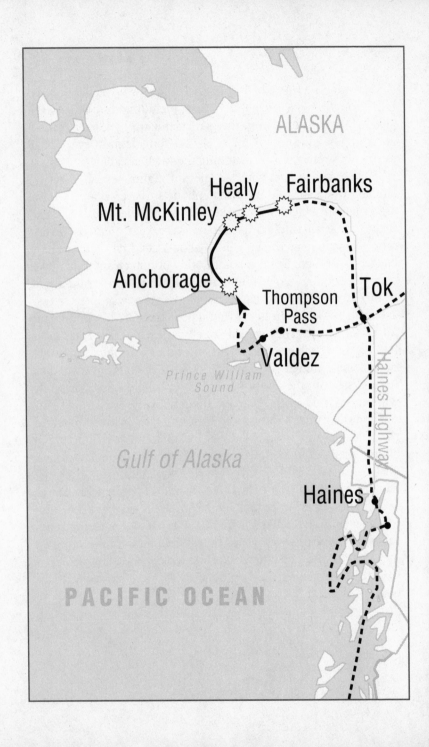

13

Father's Days

Two days to D-day, Dad's arrival. The drive north to Anchorage was stunning. Snow-covered mountains backed up against blue sky on either side of Turnagain Arm, an extension of the massive Cook Inlet. The tides this far north were extreme, with a range of up to thirty-three feet. We hoped to catch the bore tide, an abrupt rise forming a wall of water up to six feet high. The tide tables in the newspaper warned us to be on the lookout just after low tide. Somehow we miscalculated and missed it. Instead we picnicked at Beluga Point, without beluga. Anchorage, with its 250,000 residents and civilization, was just around the bend, though it felt remarkably rural this close to the city. The narrow two-lane road hugged the hillside as if hoping not to get washed out to sea. Beside us railroad tracks, the lifeline from Seward to the interior, drifted in and out of sight.

As we approached Indian Creek, the shoulders bulged from either side of the road like Joan Crawford's in a heavily padded dress. Cars were scattered everywhere, parked willy-nilly, as if the drivers had stopped suddenly for an emergency. We scanned the horizon for white whales. There were none. As we looked down from the bridge, the cause of the excitement became clear: Of course, the fish were running, and this was Alaska. We remembered friends who had once told us of building a house in Hawaii. They had been delighted to find plenty of good, hardworking craftsmen. What took some getting used to was that when the surf was up, work was out. Here the call of the wild came from fish. As we drove on, we shook our heads at our own ignorance. Next time we would know better.

As we were marveling at the accessibility of nature, the two lanes abruptly gave way to four, then six. Thoughts of fishing forgotten, familiar green highway signs loomed overhead. A divider separated us from oncoming traffic, while vehicles merged smoothly on the right. In an instant we were on an expressway in Anywhere, U.S.A. We approached the city with mixed feelings. It would be fun to get some Thai food, see Earthquake Park, and pick up a few RV supplies. Sandy was curious to look around for signs of life as he remembered it from his business trips twenty years ago. We also needed a Costco stop to get more than twenty rolls of film developed. And replenish our gourmet jelly bean supply. We did still have our priorities. Yet we seemed to have less and less use for cities.

The ease of having an RV in this city amazed us. Coming into a population center, we had girded ourselves for difficulties. I imagined pulling into Times Square to camp in the Sue, biking down to Wall Street, then up to Bloomie's and over to Central Park. A likely story. Here we located several RV parks within the city limits and chose one that was well within biking distance of everywhere we might want to go. Ninety miles of bike paths made it simple to go to and from downtown, out toward the airport to run errands, then through Earthquake Park on the water's edge. I knew this couldn't happen within fifty miles of New York. I had been, and would always be, a great defender of the Big Apple. My hometown was the only city worth living in, I thought. For energy, intensity, variety, excitement, and culture, nowhere came close. On this trip, however, for the first time I began to wonder if I really wanted to put up a fight and be tough every day for the rest of my life. My skin was so thick, I yelled at cabbies. On the other hand, I didn't really think Anchorage was a city. It felt like a big town to me. Other cities were wonderful to visit, but why would I move to Cleveland or Boise? San Francisco was beautiful, New Orleans sophisticated, but I'd take Manhattan if I wanted to go to town. Somehow since we'd opened our minds to a new life, the "where shall we live" question was had also come into play. Our friends and family were primarily in the Northeast, but not exclusively, and more and more of what we had thought of as permanent now seemed open to change. Perhaps we could live somewhere other than New York. The wheels in our minds were spinning faster about moving slower.

Even in Anchorage, however, you knew you were in Alaska. City dwellers here—unlike New Yorkers, who are mostly immune to nature—learn to thrive in the rugged climate. And there are other obvious differences between Anchorage and anywhere else, especially New York.

Things Alaskan	Things New York
Pickup trucks	525i Beemers
Dogs in pickup trucks	Teens in limos
Float planes	Corporate jets
A dog, a dock, a plane	A babe, a helipad, a jet
Salmon bakes	Chinese, delivered
Messy front yard	Lawn doctor
Real cabin style	Ralph Lauren
Woodcarvings, life size or better, chain sawn	Corporate art
Burl art	Burl Ives

Things Alaskan	Things New York
The ring of fire volcanoes	The Ring at the Met
21 hours of sunlight	The city that never sleeps
Hunting for dinner	Hunting for dinner date
Combat fishing	Combat shopping
Dog mushing	Dog walkers
Miserable roads	Miserable streets
Incredibly friendly road workers	No road workers
Drive-through espresso bars	Drive-by shootings

The advantages and disadvantages of each scrolled through my mind. We had tried living in the city during the week and in the country on weekends, not finding it very satisfying. Could there be one place that incorporated most of what we wanted?

As had become our habit, our first stop was the bookstore. I needed *F*. We parked in the K mart lot, which, legend had it, welcomed RVers to park overnight gratis. Good to know. Glad we didn't need it. As we walked toward Border's Bookstore, a chubby fellow in a suit and tie (hadn't seen one of those in a while) hustled toward us.

"Hi!" He puffed a little.

"Saw your license plates." Breathe. Breathe.

"You're sure far from home."

Was this a scam? What would he try to sell us? Was he a desperate author and no one had shown up for his book signing? "Welcome to Anchorage!"

Was he with the Chamber of Commerce? Had he read our minds and known we were thinking of moving? I felt slightly guilty that New York would find out we were even thinking of ditching her. City antennae up, we continued moving in the direction of our goal and the safety of the store.

"Hi," we allowed.

"Are you having a good time so far?" he inquired.

"Yeah, had a ball driving up. Just got to town. You live here?"

"I do. Saw your tags and knew you were a long way from home. Enjoy Anchorage."

He veered off toward his car and waved. We lamely waved back. I still had a lot to learn. This friendly-to-strangers stuff was very disorienting.

We had an interesting couple of days eating, shopping, and being tourists. One afternoon, on a break between activities, I was lounging around in my usual glam outfit of T-shirt and sweats when I logged on to our e-mail service. We were indeed part of the brave new world, for there before my eyes, from thousands of miles away, was an invitation to discuss a job. One of my former colleagues wanted to hire an editor-in-chief for one of the top publishers in America. Would I be interested? I was pleased. When were we coming home? I was flattered. When could I start work? I was very flattered. But it took all of three or four seconds to know my response. I was not interested. The freedom I felt being responsible only for the two of us, mixed with the challenge (ignoring the fear) of the unknown future, made any other answer impossible. I knew what it was I was saying no to. I knew the job inside out: the thrill of competition, the rush of being right, the enjoyment of a job well done. I also knew all about the ridiculous hours, the endless pressures, and the constantly growing publishing machine that needed feeding. As I drafted my polite thanks-but-no-thanks response, I wondered what our future would bring.

As we headed for the Anchorage airport to pick up my dad, my pop, Gerard, we did a quick drive-by of the five other flight centers in town. One, Elmendorf, was military. There was a lake for seaplanes and two very large airports for private planes, plus the regular airport. There seemed to be at least one plane per person up here and lots of air traffic problems. We had no trouble finding a parking space on the ground, however, at Anchorage International. Sandy was as eager to see Dad as I was.

The two had formed a warm, mutually respectful relationship that really was a pleasure for me. On the surface they were night and day: an eighty-year-old Jew from Berlin and a fifty-three-year-old Wasp from Michigan. But underneath they were cut from the same honest humble cloth, woven with a thread of good humor.

Dad arrived, the first person off the plane, looking a lot like an eager schoolboy off on holiday in his windbreaker and baseball cap. This would be the first time he and his wife of twenty-five years, Martha, would vacation separately. She was spending the time in New England with my recently widowed aunt. I don't think she really minded missing the excursion in the RV, and I know he didn't mind missing two weeks of sisters chatting. It was just odd seeing them apart. But it was great having him with us. He was pleased as could be that, while his friends may have gone to the Catskills for the summer, he had come to Alaska.

The three of us doubled back south to Alyeska, the largest of Alaska's six ski resorts, where we had rented a large one-bedroom apartment for Dad to shake off his jet lag and regroup. We also had a reservation at one of Alaska's best restaurants, the Double Musky. We knew a good dinner would get him on track faster than a good night's sleep, which didn't come easily at his age. One of my dad's great pleasures in life had always been fine wining and dining. After spending his career in the wine business, he had the nose and palate of a professional. As a child, I was sometimes embarrassed as he sniffed his food or wine before tasting them in restaurants. Now people just thought he was a gourmet. Supremely annoying to me was his seemingly effortlessly trim figure. By now, Sandy and I were rarely eating out. Too much Miracle Whip and too much money. Both of us were also inclined to put on weight, so we made every effort to cook and eat simply. We both loved my dad and wanted to keep him entertained and happy on this trip, so we decided it was worth a few pounds here and there. Our first night out included rack of lamb and Double Musky chocolate pie. We hated every minute of it, but hey, you do what you have to do to keep peace in the family.

In the morning we took the first gondola up the ski mountain for a good look around. It was only us and the staff. This was one of the things we had planned for Dad's visit, since it was scenic but not strenuous. The good weather was holding. The view of the valley, Turnagain Arm, and Cook Inlet was stunning. The three of us strolled around the lodge peeking into the dining rooms and looking out at the vistas. The terrain was barren at this altitude, the ground surface loose rock. After reading the warning not to pick up any unexploded artillery shells that may have been left from the previous winter's avalanche control program, we ambled outside. Together we walked up an easy trail.

As we rounded a bend, Gerard said with delight, "Look, snow!" and pointed up.

Like the old mountain goat that he was, Dad scrambled up the steep incline with me in pursuit. Sandy stood his ground and shouted at the two of us that we were nuts. As a man with a ceramic hip held in place with wood screws and two unreliable knees, he wasn't about to follow us up the treacherous, unstable incline. I chased Dad, who wouldn't stop until he had a handful of the white stuff to toss at me. I bounced one back at him. I took a picture of him, and he got one of me. We collapsed laughing side by side. It was hard to believe that I wasn't a kid anymore and that this man was eighty. Recovering our dignity, we looked back at Sandy, who glared up at us. Like two chastened children, my father and I returned to safe ground. My husband, my quiet, polite husband, told my father in no uncertain terms that he, Gerard, was not to do anything that stupid ever again. I'd never seen Sandy do that.

My father smiled and said, "Ja, ja."

This was his vacation, he seemed to say, and he was just having a little fun. Sandy shook his head as he steered us back to the security of the gondola. Instead of a wife and a father-in-law, he had been momentarily traveling with two unruly kids. Back on terra firma, we pulled into a rest stop across the inlet. A picnic lunch of smooth saga blue, garlic salami, and slabs of sourdough bread made everything right again. The magic of food.

Traveling with a third person presented an immediate challenge: There were only two front seats in the Sue. We tried rotating positions, but I got a little edgy when Dad tried to climb over the hump between the two front seats while we were moving. Sandy said I hovered too much. Mostly Dad ended up aft at the dining-room table. He pored over maps, guidebooks, and *The Anchorage Daily News.* I began to feel frustrated that he was reading about where we were and where we were going instead of looking out the window and enjoying being there. It baffled me that he could spend an entire day meandering through the Anchorage paper. There simply wasn't that much in it. But reading the paper was one of his routines. I tried to hold my tongue, but that was never one of my favorite poses.

"Pop. Look! There's the Kenai River. Can you see the incredible mountains? Left, left—look at the fish. Can you see the color of the water? Wow, how about that waterfall? Did you see how blue that glacier was? Pop, stop reading the paper—you're in Alaska! Pop! Isn't this landscape bizarre? It looks totally different all of a sudden. Don't you think it looks sort of lunar? Pop, Pop. Earth to Pop."

"Oh, I'm having a great time just being here with you kids," he said with a grin.

That wasn't enough for me. I wanted him to see what I saw, feel what I felt, be amazed at what awed and inspired me. Sandy and I traded places so I could drive. Watching the road smoothed me out. The two of them talked easily. I remembered someone once telling me, "Of course your dad knows how to push your buttons. Who do you think installed them?" Was he trying to push those buttons, or was he really having a good time? I chose to believe he was, even though I would have preferred him having a good time my way.

Over the next two weeks we covered fifteen hundred miles and built as many memories. We spent three days in torrential rains at Homer-on-the-spit (which was practically in the ocean to begin with). One night we introduced Dad to camping in the woods, a totally new experience for him. In compensation we planned a later night at a fancy hotel's plush RV park, complete with a soak in a hot tub followed by an elegant restaurant dinner. He even got to experience a night in a remote lodge with no phone, TV, or electricity. There were two boat tours and a series of great meals. We took in all the sights: from puffins and whales to volcanoes and glaciers to fabulous views of elusive Denali, the highest mountain in North America. After a bumpy day or two, we rewrote our rhythm from two part to three and got in the groove.

In the midst of all this fun, Pop woke up one morning and sounded like hell.

"I'b fine," he insisted nasally, "I'b fine."

When he didn't rally for dinner, we became concerned. Our next six days were to be spent in Denali National Park and Preserve, in the RV, in the woods, quite literally in the middle of nowhere. Instead we found him a cabin and parked the RV outside like a hovering mother whale. In the morning he had a fever and coughed. Each of us, thinking our own thoughts and not wanting to frighten the other, became very quiet. We were 238 miles from Anchorage, 120 miles from Fairbanks, and 4,647 miles from his doctor, his wife, and his familiar surroundings. I thought that if something serious was wrong, the results might be too awful to consider. Pop continued to insist he was fine, but later in the morning he wanted a second opinion from a doctor.

This was not *Northern Exposure*—there was no doctor in town. In fact, there was surprisingly little in the way of a town at the entrance to Denali, a major tourist attraction. A couple of hotels and saloons. There was no doctor. It was Saturday. We looked in our guidebooks and followed the instructions. We called the state police. We waited anxiously while they did whatever they did. They advised us to go to the medical facility at

Healy, someone would meet us there. We drove north. It was the quietest ten miles of the trip.

The clinic in Healy, population 487, was on the second floor of the Tri-Valley Community Center, attached to the volunteer fire department. As we climbed the stairs, we could hear that another patient, clearly in more dire straits, had arrived ahead of us. We followed the sound, and a friendly husky greeted us at the clinic door. Inside, a commotion of people darted back and forth to an examination room. The moaning woman quieted down after what I assumed was an injection of some sort. In the corner of the waiting room, an assortment of kids' toys testified to the fact that the whole community was served here. Though we had only just arrived, a woman who introduced herself as Sue appeared and apologized for keeping us waiting. She asked which of us was the patient and could he please fill in a brief form. Someone would be with us as quickly as possible, she informed us, then left. There was an amazing calm about the place now. We almost forgot why we were there. Sue returned, collected the paperwork, and busied herself at a desk. We read the magazines that were lying about. Most of them had to do with medicine or the outdoors. After twenty minutes or so, she said the doctor was ready for Dad. He winked at us as he followed her to one of the exam rooms. "I really do feel fine now," he said. Proximity to doctors always had that effect.

Having lost my mother when I was young, in a corner of my brain I always tried to imagine how my father's death would come about—to steel myself, I suppose, against that pain. Another part of me refused to dwell on the subject, so I'd never let my mind finish working out the possibilities. While I waited at the clinic in Healy, Alaska, flipping nervously through the same magazine several times, I told myself this was not the way. I repeated it like a mantra.

Shortly, a big bearded fellow appeared in the doorway of the examination room. He looked more like a mountain man than a medicine man, but it was a look that inspired confidence nonetheless. In fact, he cheerfully told us, he was a physician's assistant who lived in Fairbanks and was on call at Healy. In Alaska, given the vast distances and many potential hazards, medical personnel at all levels are trained to perform many on-site emergency procedures. In addition, they write and in many cases fill prescriptions on a limited basis. He marveled at what good shape Dad was in and said he wasn't worried about his condition. He gave him a bottle of cough medicine and a prescription for antibiotics in case there was any worsening of the cough. We could come back and get the pills here, since there was no drugstore. He gave us his home phone number and said to call anytime, day or night, if we felt Dad wasn't getting better. At that point we all felt better but decided Dad should be in a hotel room rather than the RV. Good thing too, since the temperature went down to twenty-nine degrees that night.

More than anything, Dad wanted to see a bear. As we drove into Denali, we saw a family of moose feeding by the side of the road. They were huge and beautiful, brown and fuzzy. Up ahead were herds of caribou, majestic and bold. But no bear. Dad's hotel was on the perimeter of the park, while we were at the Savage River Campground at Mile 13. Unfortunately, private vehicles were allowed to drive along the park road only up to Mile 14.8. The only way to the interior, to the grizzlies, was an eleven-hour jaunt on a rickety schoolbus, which we all deemed inappropriate for campers with coughs. Dad accepted the quarantine gracefully. Sandy and I submitted to the hairy ride and did see grizzlies. In fact, old eagle-eyed Sandy spotted them first, way in the distance. We got a glimpse of the north face of Denali between the clouds—and mighty tired butts from the unkind road.

At our campground that night, a ranger gave a talk around the campfire about talking to grizzlies. First, try to avoid contact. Store food in hard-sided vehicles or bear-safe canisters. Don't surprise a bear: make noise on the trail, especially if you're downwind. Stay away from cubs, even if you think they're alone, since chances are the mother is nearby. If you actually come upon one (or if one comes upon you), the park policy is something like this:

1. Wave your extended arms over your head, increasing your apparent size and letting the animal know you are not part of its usual diet.

2. Reinforce that message by speaking to it in a calm voice. Say, "Hey, bear. Hey, bear."

3. As you do this, stand still. Do not run. Running will activate the bear's chase instinct. It may sniff at you.

4. The bear will probably lose interest in you.

5. On the other hand, if it arches its back, paws the ground, and prepares to charge, play dead. Never run.

There was a lively discussion about the last point. Some people had been previously advised to play dead only in the case of brown bears but to fight back if they were pursued by a black bear. I wondered if I could will myself to faint.

We collected Dad in the morning and were cheered to learn he was hungry. Over a bacon-and-egg breakfast, we passed our recently acquired advice on to Pop, who found the idea of talking to bears highly amusing. From then on we gave each other the "Hey, bear" wave regularly. He spent most of the next few days holed up in his hotel while it rained, meeting other tourists. We'd see him between our excursions. The weather hardly mattered to us as we rafted down the Nenana River. (The water temperature had soared up to thirty-six degrees Fahrenheit.) As the day of his departure grew closer, we drove up to Fairbanks. Still not feeling great, he urged us to go off on our own. It was disquieting that he bowed out of the paddle wheel tour, since it involved only sitting. When he begged off dinner, I got really nervous again, though he insisted he was only tired. Seeing him off the next day, I was worried but relieved. He'd soon be home in his own bed, able to see his own doctor and wife. We waved a melancholy "Hey, bear" as he walked toward the plane.

Later that night we called him. He sounded absolutely fine, peppy and excited that he had spent two wonderful weeks with "the kids" in Alaska. Parents. Go figure.

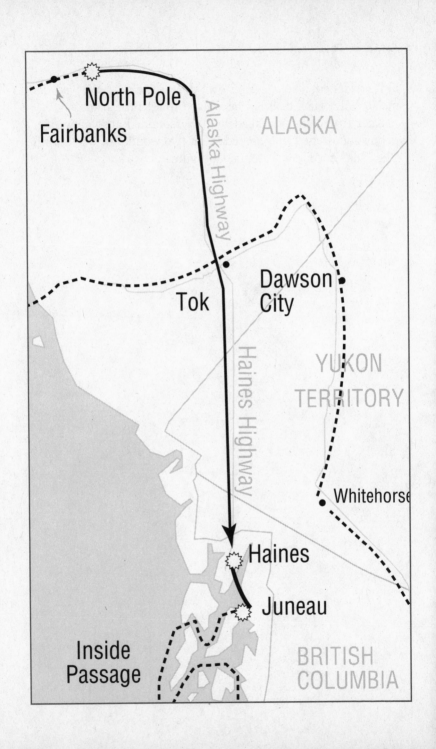

14

Personal Effects

We were in the Santa World parking lot in North Pole, Alaska. I gazed up at a thirty-foot-high statue of the man himself. Thinking about whether I'd been naughty or nice, I reviewed the past year in my mind. The previous fall I'd been running full steam ahead: appointments from breakfast through dinner, thirty-five phone calls a day, sixty-five hours a week, forty-nine weeks a year. It had now been four and a half months since I told my boss I was quitting, three months since my last day of work. Sandy and I continued to love being together, we had seen incredibly beautiful parts of the natural world, and I felt a certain fluid openness replacing rigid judgments. I still got a tremendous jolt of pleasure when I saw a book I'd been involved with in a store. We had no doubt that we loved books and publishing, but we wondered how to apply what we knew to what we didn't know. How could we mutate our years of experience and success into a future life that would be as challenging and satisfying as our careers had once been in the past? Did we truly want to get out of the fast lane, or were we aiming to merge onto the info highway from a new location? We'd been having a great time on the road for nearly nine weeks. But this wasn't a way of life—or was it? We met plenty of people who were "full timers," having traded their homes with foundations for those with wheels.

I looked up to the jolly man in red for inspiration. I believe Santa smiled. Keep on truckin', he seemed to say. I had always liked the expression "When the student is ready, the teacher appears." Maybe we could modify it to "When the worker is ready, a business appears."

I made a mental list of ways I'd changed.

Once upon a time I used to dash out of the office for twenty minutes or so between meetings to have my nails done. I loved the elegant polished look it brought to my sturdy square hands. I grew my nails as long as humanly possible, and then if tragedy struck and one broke, the professionals would glue, wrap, or otherwise cure it. Keeping all ten the same length was something of a neurotic obsession at nailworld. Though I missed the pleasant Korean manicurists, whose language I did not understand but whose chatter and grace during the minutes of respite I spent with them was a gift, I now managed to keep all twenty toes and fingers neat myself. Clever me.

Instead of torturing myself to get up and go to the gym at six o'clock three days a week, I did a series of stretches and exercises daily, plus whatever outdoor activity was available. My back, which had given me trouble for years, clutched only once: when Dad was sick. Portable stress.

I started drinking coffee again after eight years. One cup in the morning, for warmth. My diet Coke addiction eased up, however, to a couple a day instead of a couple of six-packs.

I traded in my purse for a fanny pack.
Lipstick for Chap Stick.
Perfume for Off!
Pocket change for pocket knife.
Subway map for trail maps.
House keys for Sue keys.
London Fog for Gore-Tex.
Umbrella for hood.
Silk blouses for cotton turtlenecks.
Heels for hiking boots.

————————

The single most liberating thing I did was to stop carrying. I went from being a record schlepper to the Queen of England. First as a student, then as an editor, I had always carried: backpacks, briefcases, and extra canvas bags on weekends, loaded with books, manuscripts, proposals, and magazines. I would buy pretty little pocketbooks, only to store them on the top shelf of my closet, unused, because they couldn't hold enough. Now I loved not carrying. The multipocketed vest, and maybe a fanny pack for water, was my limit. My hands were free for snapping photos, holding on to Sandy, or examining the weird rocks I picked up. Plus, I no longer listed to oné side from shoulder bag abuse. I felt incredibly light and free.

Although we had loved having Pop with us, we were also glad to get back to our own syncopated duet rhythms. Sandy still made coffee while I slept, and I tended to push further when we hiked or biked. (I was always positive there was something un-utterably fabulous just around the bend.) Yet we balanced each other out. He was more even tempered, though my "moods" were smoothing out too. Perhaps I hadn't been the sweetest of companions when I was stressed out all the time. He ate more vegetables and "used food," and I went to bed earlier than at home to keep him company. There were very few sources of conflict: it seemed that life in Alaska was as obvious as the massive mountains around us.

The roads, however, hadn't gotten any better during our visit. Taking turns at the wheel, we hit some rough stretches. It was 653 miles from Fairbanks to Haines. At least a third of that was driven, by virtue of conditions, at twenty-five miles per hour. We had fun nonetheless. The weather had turned clear again, allowing us to see the beauty all around us, although the thermometer couldn't seem to rise much past fifty during the day. We considered going up to the Arctic Circle, a couple of hundred miles beyond Fairbanks, for no other reason than to say we'd been there. The Arctic Ocean was only 299 miles beyond that, a tempting siren calling us to meet her. To get there, we learned, we'd have to take the Dalton Highway, originally the North Slope Haul Road, built by and for the oil companies during construction of the pipeline. There were very few service stations—three, to be exact—along the way. They catered to big rigs. Rigs that made Susie look like a VW Bug by comparison. If we blew a tire, say, it might just have to be imported from who knew where. The highway ended at Deadhorse (no doubt the original travelers had arrived in just that condition), two miles shy of the sea. Access roads beyond that, I read, were controlled by the oil companies, permission to use granted at their discretion. Not an inviting policy. Having become accustomed to the regular dirt roads of Alaska, we paid attention when we were told a road was *really* poor and not recommended for RVs. Only twenty-eight miles north of Fairbanks, it already became gravel. Beyond that, it was anybody's guess. Taking rental cars that way was discouraged. I regretted that we hadn't known enough about Alaska in advance to plan to spend time flying into the interior.

Having reached our outer limits, our northernmost point in this adventure was Fairbanks. Just shy of sixty-five degrees north latitude, it lies as far north of New York as Guatemala is south. I was ever more awestruck by the size and scope of the Great Land. At Fairbanks, we were 2,300 miles north of Seattle and still nearly 500 miles south of Prudhoe Bay. Nome, two and a half hours by air, was 500 miles to the west. That's a rough guess, since no road goes out that way along which to measure. Fairbanks felt like a point of entry into a wilderness within a wilderness. It is Alaska's second largest city, though with a population of only thirty thousand, a few strip malls, and a fading 1950s downtown, it reminded us of many of the disappearing upstate New York and New England villages.

On our way out of town, we passed an outfitter we had first noticed in Valdez called the Prospector. This time we stopped in. What better place than this gateway to the outback to find a genuine unadulterated original un-yuppified apparel store. Their motto, "Outfitting the Alaskan Lifestyle," sounded good to me. Their extraheavy flannel shirts felt divine. These were the kind that would keep us warm at ten below, not simply make us look cute sitting around a ski lodge. The store had an authentic warehouse look and feel, not the kind now intentionally reproduced by major chains at malls everywhere. Dozens of varieties of socks, for instance, in several thicknesses and lengths, covered one wall. They were made of materials engineered not only to keep your toes warm and dry but to make sure you came home with all of them. The place offered a fascinating visual display of self-sufficiency, from my favorite garish pink and silver salmon pixie lures, to the portable smokers in which to cure the catch, to the freeze-dried bags of lasagna in the event the fishing was lousy. There was a friendly no-nonsense manner about the people who worked there as well. Sandy wanted a turtleneck to wear under the shirts we were buying, and we found a wide variety, including some that were actually underwear and priced a bit lower. The one he liked, clearly a regular shirt, had no price tag, but since he mentioned how he would wear it, it was priced as underwear. If something was to be worn as underwear, well then, it ought to be priced as underwear. Practical people, those Alaskans.

The journey south began: through North Pole (not *the* geographic or magnetic North Pole, but a town named by a clever developer with a novel marketing idea) and Delta Junction, on our way to catch a ferry in Haines for the lower forty-eight. On the way we passed through Tok again, but this time it looked familiar. It was the first time in two months we were somewhere we had been before. It felt good to have our bearings: we knew Bob would be at the hardware store and that Cleta and Dave's restaurant, the Gateway Salmon Bake, was down the road. We were delighted that the bakery that had such good pastries hadn't yet closed for the season. Even though nothing there had changed, we now saw the town's charm and felt as if we had absorbed some sense of how Alaskans feel about their home. Some of our New York edge had worn off, and we felt the warmth of this small community. The towns may not have been cute and manicured, but they were comfortable and welcoming. We tried to imagine Tok in winter, when the temperature can reach minus seventy. Last year the first snow fell on September 10 and never left. We eagerly paid another visit to our favorite salmon bake, then headed on.

This part of the Alaska Highway took us back through some very remote stretches of the Yukon. A nasty rainstorm turned the road-in-progress to mud. I anxiously scanned the map and guidebooks for a place to spend the night. We both needed to stop. Three hundred and nineteen miles from Fairbanks, we landed at Beaver Creek, Yukon Territory, population 106. As usual, it was good to be home in the RV. It was an odd place, however. This little hamlet had sprung up like a mushroom out of nowhere. The road bulged a bit, and a Westmark Inn had been planted. Built simply out of wood (though not the log structure one would hope for), it was an ideal stopping point for happy cruisers as they were lugged by bus from the port at Skagway up to Whitehorse or Dawson and beyond. I liked the slogan in their ad: "The highway traveler will find comfort and convenience at our modern rendition of the traditional road-house." I found Cuervo Gold and nachos and was perfectly thrilled.

The next day we passed through Burwash Landing, along Kluane Lake. I remembered all the nodding heads when the Kluane First Nation singer had announced this was his hometown, back in Whitehorse. Now we also knew where Burwash was. It felt good to be familiar and think we knew someone here. We fell in line, like the good tourists we were, and bought a cache of Native goods: moccasins for Cindy and Claire, a hat for me, beads for Eva, and booties for the Butler babies, twins who were expected to make their debut in New York after the New Year. Burwash was not much of a town—a museum and a few buildings. But the location was unbeatable: huge peaks of the Kluane and St. Elias ranges poked out between the clouds. As we drove south, hugging Kluane Lake on our left, we passed the site of Destruction Bay, one of the original relay stations for the building of the highway. While the population was under a hundred, they managed to sponsor a fishing derby every July. A modern motel and several RV parks aided and abetted tourists on the make for trout or glacial flightseeing. In Haines Junction we fortified ourselves with several excellent pastries, both savory and sweet, and swung by British Columbia on our way to the Alaskan coast.

The weather brightened again as we headed south, though I was glad to snuggle into my Prospector shirt. Golden leaves highlighted the ever-sharpening image of the sunshine-lit landscape. The blacktop curved, dipping and rising like a band of wet black licorice. We arrived in the harbor town of Haines as the sun was setting and realized an awful truth: Summer was over. It was getting dark early—nine o'clock.

We spent several days exploring the area by bike, on foot, and in the RV, fueled by fine buttermilk sticks from the Chilkat Bakery. It was an exquisite spot for a town, nestled in the fjord with a safe harbor. The saving grace for the town, we thought—though the residents might have preferred otherwise—was that the cruise ships didn't stop here. Development maintained an organic pace. Up and across the bay at Skagway, we heard it was all for the touristos, a group we indignantly and increasingly separated ourselves from. Haines had a pristine feeling, as if it had grown to its current stature of fifteen hundred souls by its own merits. There were several parks that afforded fine fishing, camping, and opportunities to stare at nature. Totally unimaginable to me several months earlier, I spent one enjoyable lunchtime sitting by the edge of a lake watching for bald eagles. I actually think my jaw dropped when I saw my first one cruise onto the upper reaches of a tall pine. It was like seeing a legend.

We were, luckily for our nearest and dearest, able to buy some more gifts here. A special favorite was the T-shirt that said:

ALASKAN MEN. THE ODDS ARE GOOD, BUT THE GOODS ARE ODD

The Native crafts were among the most beautiful we had seen. There were wonderfully colorful beaded wall hangings, stone carvings, and leather goods. By the time we packed up to leave, we had to make several boxes in Sue's "basement" available for storage of the trinkets. Now I knew why beads had once been such useful currency. They're easy to pack.

*   *   *

We boarded the M.V. *Columbia* near midnight. The 418-foot flagship of the Alaska Marine Highway fleet was a city in the making. With balletlike grace dozens of vehicles were directed into position on the car deck. In keeping with the rugged nature of the state, sleeping was permitted anywhere on the vessel (except in a vehicle). Tenters were invited to camp on the solarium deck. We opted for a cabin. It had the basics: bunk beds, a shower, a head, and a washstand. We yearned for the Sue, two decks down—we were allowed to visit twice a day when the purser announced a car deck call. A village of six hundred or so folks settled in for this night and the three to follow. The air was cold and the sky inky. We saw stars for the first time since we'd left Michigan. Quietly we slipped out of port, in great contrast to the bump, clang, and thud with which we'd entered the state. I thought of other trips we'd been on and our routine of planning of where we'd go next as we went home. As we made for Washington State through the inside passage, I felt sorry to be leaving this wild territory and wondered how soon we could come back. We'd covered only four thousand miles here, and there was so much more to see.

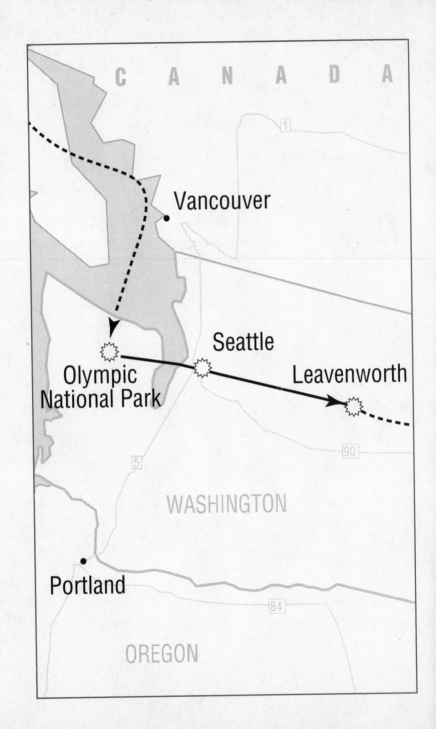

15

Half Full

Back in the U.S., back in the U.S., back in the U.S. of A. My version of the Beatles' lyric thrummed in my head as we landed. Arriving at the dock in Washington after a quick side trip to Vancouver Island left us no doubt we were back in civilization. Noise, road signage, advertisements, hustle, bustle. We had radio reception to beat the band. The towns on the Olympic Peninsula teemed with people. We felt like foreigners, speaking a language of our own. Hey, bear. When we called my folks, they rejoiced—admittedly selfishly—that since we'd always said we'd be home in plenty of time for Thanksgiving, our trip was half over. It made me terribly sad.

The Alaska portion of our trip felt so singular to me. It had a shape, texture, and flavor all its own. Moreover, it had a purpose and goals. We had simply driven every passable road in the state. Now there were endless choices that had to be made. The options were innumerable here in the lower forty-eight. We could go south through Oregon and then head east. Or we could continue south to California and then figure it out. Or we could go directly east through Washington to Idaho and into Montana—but should we cross through the panhandle and head for Missoula, or take back roads and aim for Bozeman? The maps, guidebooks, and atlases strewn all over the Sue were useless until we determined where we wanted to go. There were too many paved roads that could be taken. The truly carefree days seemed over.

It felt as if we had to prove something to someone. I wasn't sure what and to whom, but I felt we were in the visible part of the hemisphere again, back on the scope. I called a friend on the West Coast, who verified this for me. She wanted me to know lots of work was available, if I was interested. No, but thanks anyway. Maybe this was the kind of pressure I always created for myself. Maybe this was the part where we were supposed to figure out what to do with the rest of our lives. I felt a slight squeeze in my chest. Maybe it was the readily available newspapers and phone lines that put me back in the plan-your-work-and-work-your-plan mode. Maybe some primal sense that summer was over, time to get serious and back to school, was closing in on me. Maybe, maybe, maybe. I definitely did not like this queasy feeling. It had been so easy to just live, in Alaska, to simply let myself be. I loved absorbing the natural world there, exploring with all my senses. Now I felt edgy, anxious about what we would do, wondering how it would be. There were so many choices. Driving would help. Motion was a good thing.

We sought to avoid the throngs by going into Olympic National Park, as if it were a safe haven offering us a temporary moratorium from the press of humanity. It was just the place to go to lift our spirits as well. A natural dream palace, a northern jungle built of ancient trees laced with mosses, it was mysterious but not frightening. Setting up camp amid the giant fir trees made us feel minuscule, a surefire wake-up call to the insignificance of my anxieties. Early the next day we took a hike. As we traversed the soft trail of pine needles, meeting no other human being as we went, I wouldn't have been at all surprised to see an elf or a gremlin. The rich moist greens were intoxicating after the harshness of the North. Had I seen a gnome (I elected to think it would be in the shape of our recently departed friend who published a book on the subject, Ian Ballantine), I would not have been at all taken aback. As we walked along, without interruption from man or beast, our anxieties were soothed. Increasingly powerful swords of light cut through the morning mist as we walked the enchanted woods. Maybe King Arthur dwelled here. We sat on a log bench to eat our lunch of apples, cheese, and bread, then made our way back to camp utterly refreshed, ready to meet whatever humans might be at the Sol Duc Hot Springs.

If the walk hadn't sane-itized me, the waters surely would have. The naturally occurring springs surfaced at 135 degrees and were cooled in four pools to temperatures ranging from 75 to 105. Once again we were sure that happy ions filled the air or water around us, because not a soul among us seemed discontent. After a good soak I reconstituted myself and my opinion of the trip by deciding the glass was half full, not half empty. The next two months would be just as exciting as the last. Different, not less. We determined that they would be the beginning of the next chapter in our lives, not the end of the trip of a lifetime.

Driving along the coastline in the predictable rain and fog of the Pacific Northwest proved disappointing and frustrating, so we headed inland for Mount Rainier. We seemed to zig and zag back and forth through the seasons. In Denali it had felt nearly like winter, while later, in Vancouver, it had been summery. Now there were hints of early fall in the trees. Darkness was coming earlier each day, it seemed, pushing us inside and reminding us that autumn was not to be stopped. We made a little home-renovation stop, buying two reading lamps to brighten the evenings and a huge deep red mum plant. While we drove, we kept the mum in the shower. When we arrived somewhere for the night, we placed it outside beside our steps. It gave a funny Martha-Stewart-was-here look to nature.

At 14,000 feet, Rainier is the tallest mountain in Washington, though it's 6,000 feet shy of Denali, against which we now compared everything. The mountain was a magnificent sight as it rose quickly before us, showing off her white shoulders and cap. Even though there were people here (the campsites were all taken), I felt at ease. In fact, on a stroll through the campground, we admired one RV that had slide-outs (sections of the vehicle that expanded once it was parked) and boldly asked the owners for a tour. A handsome couple from Nebraska in their early fifties, they were happy to oblige. We traded brief road histories. They told us they had retired, sold their home, and been on the go since the spring. Using one of their daughters' addresses as a mail drop, they were footloose and delighted with life as a couple after years of parenting. Inside, their home looked lavish and large to us. The living portion was thirty-five feet long, expanding in both the bedroom and living areas to twelve feet wide in places. Several pieces of furniture were loose (the dining table and chairs, for instance)—a miracle to us, who had become accustomed to everything being fixed. The bathroom was elegant, with both a stall shower and a tub. The home could be disconnected from a pickup truck, giving them transportation of a smaller kind when they wanted it. We asked whether they had a plan for the upcoming months. Beyond a trip to California to visit family, life was going to be a surprise, they said. No more plans, thank you, no more schedules. The only plan was to move when they felt like it, stop when they wanted. They were surely happy campers. We thanked them for their hospitality and mused whether we could do that. It certainly had some appeal.

We signed up for a hike with a ranger, who told us a remarkable thing: When a tree's life is threatened, stressed by the elements of fire, drought, or other calamity, it twists beneath its bark to reinforce and make itself stronger. On the surface this new inner strength may not be visible, for the bark often continues to give the same vertical appearance. Only when the exterior is stripped away, or when the tree is felled, are its inner struggles revealed. How incredibly human, I thought. The image of the twisting tree stayed with me. That night Sandy and I talked about the parallels between the tree's powers of adaptation and human experience. I believed that hardship could strengthen the spirit, and that, conversely, it was rare to find someone with great depth of emotion and empathy who had faced no hardships or spiritual challenges. I kept thinking about those trees, twisting what seemed to be fixed, readjusting the core to keep the head skyward.

*   *   *

Refreshed and stimulated, we braced ourselves for what we thought of as our first real city visit. Seattle lay appropriately enshrouded in fog as we approached her from the south that morning. I looked forward to taking Sandy to the Pike Place Market, a treasure trove of fresh produce, meats, fish and seafood, bakeries, Italian specialty foods, and all kinds of arts and crafts. I'd been there once before, when I was in town for a sales meeting eighteen months earlier. On that visit I had viewed Seattle from the shiny side—the east side of the market. Elegant hotels, tall office towers, and trendy restaurants were what I saw. I had paid homage to the original Nordstrom's, my favorite department store. It has a wonderful shoe department and offers old-time service. Now, as Sandy drove the Sue along the waterfront, we saw the city from her rear flank. The port was busy with steamers and barges. Stevedores and seamen worked, hoisting and hefting. It was a gray, grimy sight. I was reminded that this was the port where hundreds of thousands of hopefuls had gathered to obtain passage north to the goldfields in Alaska in 1898. Rounding a bend, we saw the scene upgraded to tourist class, with a pier full of gift shops, a ferry terminal, and a restored trolley line. We arrived behind the market before nine. There was ample parking and easy access to the city, up the hill to our right. Once again I mused about finding parking for the Sue in Manhattan near any of the waterfront attractions. My hometown has a lot to answer for in that regard.

Welcome, hungry campers! Heaven was upon us. Though we hadn't suffered for lack of comestibles, the sight of all this edible glory under one roof was nearly too much for my heart to bear. Built in several stages, the market was partially indoors, partially out. First to attract us was not some exotica but simple corn, the one thing we hadn't seen all summer and craved. Farmers' stands were loaded with fruits and vegetables of all kinds. Craftsmen tended to be found upstairs near the street, while the gift and other shops were located deep within the building at various levels. We found prosciutto and ripe melon to go with it, stocked up on Brie, crusty bread, and of course salami. The fishmongers practically danced with their goods, in order to call our attention to their wares. In a moment of nostalgia, I bought a piece of smoked Alaskan salmon. There were jams, relishes, and vinegars of local provenance, alongside buckets of glorious fresh-cut flowers. After two hours of wandering, gazing, pointing, and paying, the crowd began to develop into a serious mob. Time for us to go and have lunch.

A friend I had worked with in New York had moved back to Seattle with his wife and baby to be closer to their families. Now he had a wonderful job as a much bigger fish in a much smaller pond. I told him I needed a Thai fix, and he suggested we meet at a pan-Asian restaurant within walking distance of the market. Over huge steaming bowls of chicken and noodles in an aromatic ginger, coconut milk, and coriander broth, we babbled about the differences between living and working in New York and Seattle. Life was easier here, but work was challenging. New friends were harder to make at this age, and old contacts were not as interested in doing business. I quizzed him about his life, about the transition, and about his wife and how she was faring, hoping for revelations. There were no miracle cures for my disease about our future—where to live or what to do. We would simply have to reinvent ourselves in our own way, in our own time. After catching up and eating our fill, we said good-bye. Sandy and I headed for literary Mecca, the Elliott Bay Bookshop, a wonderful store with friendly intelligent clerks. I found *F* and a bagful of other goodies.

Leaving the city was a nightmare of traffic jams and road

construction, but at least we were moving. I wondered if we were becoming addicted to being on the go, a sort of motion sickness in reverse: when I wasn't going anywhere, I became nauseous. I asked my husband whether he thought it was fatal. We looked at each other and grinned. We had food, we had gas, we loved each other, and we were on the road. Life was good. Except for this creepy guy in a turquoise pickup truck who kept popping up on either side of us and gesticulating. At a red light he pulled up directly under my right elbow. He opened his window. Reflexively, yet feeling somewhat defensive, I did the same. "Welcome to Washington!" he crowed. "Isn't it beautiful, hope you'll like it. Been here long? Long way from home! Bye!" The light changed, and he was gone. I was still surprised by the kindness of strangers. And a little ashamed of some of my preconceived notions of the world.

We went from zero to 4,061 feet above sea level in under three hours as we rose through the mist of the Cascades at Stevens Pass. A few miles beyond the peak, as if a veil had been lifted, the sky turned robin's egg blue, a green valley spread out ahead of us, and we came into Leavenworth, Washington. Much to our surprise, it was a Bavarian village, where even the price of gasoline was lettered in old Germanic script. There must be a bakery here, *ja*? A little strudel, perhaps? We found the last site available at a campground that looked as if Heidi might have slept there, complete with little white fences running along bright green grass and beds of blooming flowers. It seemed that tucked into the lap of the mountains, we had even found a taste of spring.

16

Greta Garbo in Last Chance Gulch

Driving across Washington was a lesson in geography, topography, and weather. We went up from damp sea level at Seattle, down the sunny eastern slope of the Cascades, across the semiarid high plains, to nearly desert conditions at the Grand Coulee Dam, and across mountain passes into Idaho, all in fewer than four hundred miles. Somewhere in there we discovered apples. It was harvest time: Jonagolds, Red Delicious, MacIntosh, and half a dozen other varieties were stacked artfully at roadside stands. Pyramids of red, gold, and green. Crates, overfull with crisp, sweet, moist fruits, stood at angles to tempt the thirsty traveler. Sandy MacGregor, true to his roots, preferred the MacIntoshes. I thought the Braeburns were great, but I fell in love with Fujis. They were, to my tongue, the perfect apple: crunchy, juicy, a little bit of tartness just after the initial burst of sugar.

The scenery changed constantly. Alpine villages mutated into neatly plowed open spaces, which gave way to raw red dirt that seemed to dry out before our eyes, finally becoming dusty desert. We were arm Rockettes, flinging our fingers out left and right; Look at this! See that? Over there! As we watched, the landscape molted.

In between set changes we tried to focus on upcoming business. After we hadn't gotten the company in Vermont, Sandy had continued to look elsewhere for opportunities. Given our complementary skills, we were convinced we had a lot to offer in the right situation. Since we'd left home, our natural inclination toward getting along well together seemed enhanced, not threatened. As the notion of working together grew more tempting, the possibility of going back into a major corporation became less likely with every mile. The farther I got from Big Biz, Inc., the more amazed I was that I had been in it for twenty-two years. While I believed that work was a good and satisfying thing, I felt a little shell-shocked that I had spent all that time growing more rigid as I molded my ways to the needs of a corporation. I also strongly doubted that I, or anyone else, had been used to the best of their ability. A frustrating, sad thought. When I first began my career, I had been enthralled with the glamour of meeting famous authors and working on their books, even though much of what I did had involved the finer points of typing and xeroxing. Still, it was important, honorable work, and I felt proud of my contributions. I felt stimulated by new ideas and by having opinions that mattered among my peers. An older friend had watched my progress with a skeptical eye. He gave me a dire warning not to get caught up in riding the merry-go-round, because I might think that the earth was moving with me, when it was really just the floor of the carousel. What was this fool talking about? I thought. It only took twenty years for me to understand. While I was spinning around so quickly, it was easy to mistake the floor for real ground. The difference was made clear to us abruptly when Sandy was fired. He had lost his job, as well as his orientation in life. While we drove, we talked about all this, and over many days and weeks, it became clear that one of the things we both felt lacking in the "new" corporate environment was a sense of community. By establishing ourselves in a new project, we hoped to find a way of life as part of a community, whether it was directly work related or simply in the place where we would live. In a few days we would be meeting in Helena with a publisher who was looking for a buyer for a majority share. Perhaps this would be "it," the purpose and place we were looking for.

* * *

Montana has been called "the last best place," and we had a hunch why. We had crisscrossed its Rocky Mountain spine several times. It was spectacularly pretty country, full of peaks and valleys, lakes and streams famous for trout fishing. There had been lots of complaining in the past few years about Ted and Jane and all the other celebrities buying up property, bringing with them an entourage of pricey art galleries and cutesy home-furnishing stores, driving up the cost of basics for the locals. To our jaded eyes, Montana looked fresh, young, and bright. True, Missoula surprised us on this visit with a new Costco. Good for developing film, bad for keeping the pace down. Bozeman had a new shopping area under construction. The trailers scattered about gave the impression that housing couldn't keep up with the boom. Perhaps nothing ever stayed the same anywhere except the complaints: A town was either growing too fast or slowly dying. It either reached a critical mass and became a city, or it returned to dust. Still, for the most part, we very much liked what we'd seen of Montana. As we were debating the merits and debits of living in Montana, on the way to our campsite we found definitive proof, and obtained photographic evidence, that bears do shit in the woods. A black bear cub was doing his business by the side of the road. Not even a thirty-foot Winnebago was going to interrupt him.

We set up camp in the woods near a stream. After scouting the area on foot, we started fixing dinner. Since our major scores at the Pike Place Market and the farm stands of Washington, the larder was well stocked. Cooking was a sport for us as much as a necessity. At times it was also an almost erotic pleasure. Tastes, textures, and temperatures of a good meal could mingle to produce alluring evenings or, in our liberated condition, idyllic afternoons. While Sandy fired up the grill, I hauled out provisions and thought about the components of meals for the sensual traveler.

Breakfast, when possible, should include a small bowl of local berries, sprinkled with sugar, if desired, and glazed in a few spoonfuls of freshest cream. Eat slowly, and play with the food in your mouth, rolling it around with your tongue till you're done.

Lunch was made for leftovers. Any kind of grilled meat can be appreciated when sliced and bedded down on some salad greens, dressed appropriately in garlic and oil. (See page 157: Garlic Dressing to Bond You to Each Other.) Lots of flavorful oil makes it all slide down nicely. My favorite lunch requires no preparation, other than shopping. Here's the recipe: Take a good sourdough roll or slab of bread. Apply a heaping spoonful of soft blue cheese; six or eight slices of crisp cold apple, preferably a Fuji; and a wedge of salami. Eat slowly, in alternating nibbles.

Dinner should be simple yet satisfying, fortifying you to live through the long (or short, if you're in Alaska) night. Always use spice and zest. Flank steak or chicken slathered in garlic/chili paste is good. Little containers of pesto last months and always make a robust pasta dish. Pork is especially good on the grill. Try this: grilled pork chops on top of a salad of red leaf lettuce, chopped radishes, tomato wedges, scallions, and cukes dressed in mayonnaise or soy sauce and ginger.

Miracle foods include *couscous*—it can be made fast. Toss in chopped leftover anything and eat hot or cold. It also stores well. *Tomatoes* can be cooked as sauce or baked and stuffed, sliced on a turkey sandwich, or with good mayo, make up a sandwich in their own right. *Bacon* is good because it makes everyone happy just to eat it these days.

Surprises: *Grilled carrots,* sliced lengthwise, marinated in salt, olive oil, and crushed rosemary, are a treat for dinner—and leftover on sandwiches, instead of tomatoes, say, for lunch. *Smoked things* are aromatic, tasty, and practical—they keep well.

Garlic Dressing to Bond You to Each Other

*In a small bowl mash a handful of garlic cloves and a teaspoon of
salt with the back of a spoon till it forms a paste.*
Add a light olive oil to it, while stirring to combine.
Flavor with raspberry vinegar, Tabasco, and black pepper.

Make a lot—it keeps well refrigerated.
If you have a blender, so much the better.

That night we started off with luscious ripe honeydew melon
slices wrapped in prosciutto—a nice salty/sweet, chewy/slippery
combination. Following that we had grilled spicy andouille sausages, steamy jasmine rice, and green salad dressed in garlic.
Dessert involved nibbling away at the pastry collection. It's a
rough life out in the wilderness.

* * *

After the ups and downs of Washington, the Sue started complaining. She increasingly objected to heights and was none too
pleased as we made our way through MacDonald Pass at 6,320
feet. The higher we climbed, the more she sputtered and
coughed, and the slower she went. She took no consolation in
the view of the valley as it spread out before us from the crest
where we stopped.

Montana's valleys are always breathtaking to me. Several
mountain ranges run north-south in this part of the state, creating huge fertile basins in between. I always thought of Barbara
Stanwyck, hands on hips, standing guard in *The Big Valley*. Unlike terrain in the East, where the mountains are gently rounded
and valleys scooped, here the peaks are younger and still jagged,
breaching the surface of the earth in a more angular fashion. The
distance between ranges allows the broad valleys to become
level, giving the eye the opportunity to imagine the curve of the
earth in the distance. We'd fallen in love with the openness of
the land and the people years before. Folks we met here were

independent, to be sure. Before we'd heard the word *militia,* we thought of that independence as a good thing, not as a euphemism, and in our experience it remained that way. There was simply a distaste for interference, whether the source was personal or professional, neighborly or governmental. It was as if everyone had come here to be alone, a state full of Greta Garbos. That seemed fine to us.

Susie breathed a sigh of relief as we coasted into Helena, the state capital. We were eager to explore the town a bit, a difficult thing in a thirty-foot truck, so we opted for a tour. The "train" went through the elegant Upper West Side with its handsome Victorian and Arts-and-Crafts-period homes built by captains of industry. It then snaked through the small downtown to the far end of Last Chance Gulch—yesterday's red light district, today's main street. It was a distance of a mile or so. Downtown was in the process of being revitalized and had several fine turn-of-the-century buildings. The capitol building and grounds were impressive in a generic way. There's nothing particularly unique or Montanan about the place. After the tour we drove around the perimeter of the town, which was depressingly like a giant strip mall. Hoping to find a town center or square, we circled twice and found none. We tried to locate the Chamber of Commerce to pick up a relocation packet. (Most towns of any size will give or sell you this handy compilation of information on industries, housing, population, climate, and the like.) The Chamber had moved, leaving no forwarding address. We used our phone (hallelujah, praise the gods of electricity, we had service at last) to get the new number, which turned out to be constantly busy. Finally we got through just as they were closing, and they did not offer to stay open the few minutes it would have taken for us to get there. It was a Friday afternoon, and, we supposed, even Chamberites have plans and lives. We were miffed anyhow.

In this cranky frame of mind, we headed for the post office, where we were hoping to pick up some mail forwarded by a friend. The envelope was there! We felt much better. When we opened it, we were shocked to find it mostly filled with the friend's own junk mail. We felt sick. Panicked about what we'd missed, what bills might be overdue, we wondered about our friend's well-being. In the parking lot we hauled out our office box and did a quick review of checks outstanding and bills paid. There was no obvious gap, so we hoped for the best, but we felt queasy anyhow. We called him, hoping he wasn't ill with some mysterious mis-filing fever. He was terribly apologetic and embarrassed. It seems he'd quit smoking that week and was a little befuddled. He promised to recheck everything, and we hung up, relieved and amused. We both used to be smokers and remembered those first few weeks after quitting, when the smoke was replaced with a mental fog. We breathed a smoke-free sigh of relief. What a weird afternoon. We headed for a campground to Garbo it, be alone, for a while.

That night we met with the publisher and his wife at a funky saloon for burgers and talk. He was a wiry fellow who immediately gave the impression of being a natural runner. His wife reminded me of my college friends, with her soft flowing batik-print clothes and long luxurious hair. The four of us seemed a comfortable mix. He gave us a brief history of the business, their roles in it, and its current condition. His books were of excellent quality. The spreadsheet looked healthy. His energy level was such that he could barely stay in his seat as he told us about his unique and aggressive distribution ideas, as well as the editorial projects he was eager to undertake. Far from the drumbeat of Manhattan, this guy had formulated plans that large publishers could only dream about executing. Because of dogged hand selling and creative marketing, he had been able to place his books in locations where books are generally not sold. Because his operation was largely localized, he could afford to cover those areas in depth. It was an exciting discussion. They drove us back to the Sue, and we agreed to meet again in the morning.

Sandy and I walked around the edge of the campground looking at the stars. It was the blackest night we'd had yet, and it was beautiful. A shooting star, so big we both saw it, left a smudge as it sailed through the sky.

The offices were large and impressive. The people we met were lovely, and speaking with them individually, we were impressed with their abilities. The publisher clearly had surrounded himself with a talented, dedicated staff. It seemed to us that things were in great shape. In fact, there didn't appear to be much we could bring to the party. His business instincts were good, and his editorial program solid. There was nothing obvious that needed fixing. He offered several ideas of how we might work together, but what became clear was that cash, not contributors, was needed. Unfortunately, we could not be the angel he needed. It was a wonderful visit, rekindling our interest in just such a business, and we promised to stay in touch. As we rode out of town, I admitted to being a little relieved. I didn't know if I would be happy as a Greta Garbo in Last Chance Gulch.

*   *   *

We went to another gulch, to the place Norman MacLean had described so well in *Young Men and Fire*. Twenty miles out of Helena, up the Missouri River, is a place named Gates of the Mountains. Lewis and Clark explored this limestone canyon in 1804. In the summer of 1949 a sudden brushfire exploded with terrible heat and roared through Mann Gulch, jumping the river. The men fighting the fire were a new team, just formed. For many of them it was their first time out. The flames were whipped by the wind, and moving with horrible speed, they trapped the men in the ravine. The most experienced among them tried to convince the others to go back down into the fire with him, to stand in a place that had already been burned. He said it was their only hope—they could never outrun the blaze. Yet logic and the thirst for oxygen drove them up the mountain, where they perished. It's a quiet spot now, the wind whooshing through the tall grass. A fitting memorial to the dead.

We followed the water south to Canyon Ferry Lake and a

harbor filled with sailboats. The clanging of the halyards against masts reminded us of the sounds of the Caribbean. My name-sake hurricane was just then battering the Virgin Islands, and we hoped our friend Captain Gwen was in a hole as snug as ours.

17

Company's Coming

In the morning we found ourselves in Townsend, Montana, where everything looked pretty much as it had for the last fifty or sixty years. Not only that, it seemed they'd forgotten to raise their prices. Surrounded by cowboys, we had an A-1 breakfast at the corner restaurant: two eggs, two pieces of bacon, two sausages, two pancakes, two bucks. These were not miniaturized portions, either. What a treat. Just the sort of place we always hoped to find but rarely did.

Appropriately fortified, we took the chance of getting lost down a winding back road. We bobbed and weaved through a narrow canyon dotted with tumbleweed and an occasional llama. They are becoming quite common in the West, though I always thought they looked kind of goofy and out of place. Our mystery tour led toward the Lewis and Clark caverns. Oddly, the entrance was way above us. To get there, we drove up to a parking lot on a mile-high mesa, then hiked up another three hundred feet on a dusty path in the noonday sun for three-quarters of a mile in order to get to the entrance. We figured this was a test to weed out the lazy, easily deterred, or unfit. Since parts of the tour involved navigating on your butt, crawling on hands and knees, and climbing stairs while stooped, self-elimination seemed a kind way to do things. Sandy was a sport to accompany me, since he really couldn't care less about caves.

For some reason I could not identify, I was always attracted to caverns. The constant climate and the odd formations of varying textures intrigued me. More than that, the feeling of being close to something primitive inside these ancient "chambers" thrilled me. The Lewis and Clark caverns were the most dramatic I'd ever seen. Huge stalagmites and stalactites, slick with moisture and smooth with age, surrounded us. Rooms of varying sizes, from closet to chapel, were filled with formations in myriad shapes and colors. In the semidarkness stone took on the features of flesh as the guide pointed out witch's, lovers', and papal profiles. There was a pleasant creepy-crawly feeling in the caves, though when the lights went off, I shuddered with real fear. Everyone stood still, and even the children hushed. Was this part of the routine, or had something gone awry? The moment before the guide spoke next lasted forever. This was not the kind of darkness one's eyes adjusted to after a while, allowing for a dim perception of shape and depth. This was eternal pitch. The chilly temperature of the caves seemed enhanced, the moisture on my skin more pronounced as my sight was suddenly removed. I felt a prickly sensation where my scalp meets my face. Our guide remedied the situation, though he said he was puzzled about why it had happened. At the exit the sunlight was blinding, and the air remarkably fresh.

In compensation for being dragged through slime, I offered to take my hubby to our favorite Montana restaurant, Sir Scott's Oasis in Manhattan, our home away from home. Dinner at Sir Scott's was once described as "the defining beef moment" in the life of a food writer. So it had been for us when we were first there, four years earlier. From the outside it had looked like the kind of place we wouldn't likely hang out in. Set across from the railroad tracks on the two-block main drag of town, a cheesy neon sign hung over its makeshift storefront bar. Good place for a brawl, I'd thought. In the rear was a rough dining room. The steaks, however, had been every bit as divine as we'd heard, tastier than any I'd ever had. Since we'd been there last, business had boomed. A major expansion had transformed Sir Scott's into a large restaurant with a small bar off to the side. The eat-till-you-bust concept of dining remained intact, however. A pile of crackers and butter, soup and salad, a huge rib-eye steak, fries, and an ice cream sundae reminded me of the good old days before I knew the names of those demon sisters, *calorie* and *cholesterol*. We probably should have walked it off, but we preferred the Bozeman Hot Springs soak/melt-it-off approach.

* * *

We needed to do some housecleaning and shopping. Company was coming in at two o'clock that afternoon on the Delta flight at Gallatin International. Sandy's daughter, Cindy, and her boyfriend, John, were spending the first part of their vacation with us before taking off on their own. We were really looking forward to spending some R and R together. Six years earlier Cin had started her own business, with one client, as a computer graphic designer. Talented and driven, she had no interest in going to work in a corporation. We needled her about getting a real job, prodded her about getting benefits, poked her about having insurance. Polite but firm, she went about work her own way, inventing it as she went. Now she had more customers, worked her own hours (too many), in her own way (perfectionism runs in families, I'm told), with two full-time employees and a floating staff of free-lancers. We were incredibly proud of her but spent increasingly less time together. We were delighted when she and John said they wanted to meet up with us.

In New York picking someone up at the airport is a stroke short of lunacy, an offense for which you can be committed to a nearby asylum on the say-so of the skycap. It can take an hour or two just to get to the airport. Parking your car presents the risk of having it broken into or simply not being there upon your return. Finally, due to security, passengers can no longer be met at the gate. Why bother? When someone comes to visit in New York, they get the message right away: If you can't get into town on your own, don't bother coming. Elsewhere, I had discovered, visiting was still a complete and relatively pleasant event. At Gallatin airport, the parking attendant kindly showed us which part of the lot was best suited to a thirty-foot vehicle. As we stood at the gate (one of four), waiting for Cindy and John's plane to arrive, a sense of anticipation built. When an announcement was made that the flight was delayed, we waiters flocked to the bar, then migrated back just in time to welcome our loved ones. (Any leftover drinks were accommodatingly re-poured into paper cups.) With the exception of my dad and our friend in Seattle, we had seen no one we knew in over two months. When these two familiar faces walked into the terminal (through the fresh mountain air across the tarmac, not through a hermetically sealed jetway), we were thrilled. It was good to be with family.

Ten or fifteen years earlier, I had worked on a series of books about the then-trendy subjects of single parenting, quality time, and stepfamilies. I had related to all of them from the perspective of the child: after my mother died, I'd been raised by my dad—now called a single parent—who had spent as much (quality) time with me as he could. When I was in college and he married Martha, we became an all-German-Jewish-American stepfamily. She and I both hated the term *stepmother* and silently agreed never to use it. She was introduced as my dad's wife or, more commonly, as Martha, as if it were a title. As I approached forty, I married Sandy, his son and daughter, Alex and Cindy, becoming my stepchildren. They were in their twenties. When Alex married Fiona, a young woman from Britain whose mother was from Gibraltar, I became an in-law. Now John was part of the mix. An amiable Italian-American who showed tremendous appreciation for my cooking efforts, he added a generous amount of good nature and well-honed muscles to our brew.

Now I had an extended nuclear multicultural multigenerational stepfamily. It occurred to me that I could now have read those same books from the parental point of view, if the kids had been twenty years younger. I wondered at the oddity of modern life.

We traveled with Cindy and John to two magical places. The first was Yellowstone, where we'd seen our first buffalo. It had been right after the film *Dances With Wolves* came out, and we were overwhelmed with the urge to call them *tatanka* in the stumbling, stammering, heavily dentalized style of Kevin Costner. In Yellowstone we took Cindy and John to the bizarre Mammoth Hot Springs, where white, aqua, and copper-colored minerals have dripped down layers of rocks for centuries, creating a hillside reminiscent of a wedding cake that ran. Multicolored terraces, bubbling with pools of steaming sulfurous waters, climb the side of the mountain. (Watching Cindy's face, alive with expressiveness and delight, as she took in and enjoyed something I liked so much made me regret that I hadn't been there to see her grow up. Then again, I hadn't had to make her do her homework or clean her room either.) At the center of this scene was a regal male elk. Perched on a warm central ledge, his head held high despite a crown of heavy antlers, it was his favorite time of year—mating season. All around him, on various levels, were his obedient harem of females and their young offspring. When the mood moved him, he would rise, stretch his snout skyward, and bugle, letting all the ladies know what he had in mind. He'd stomp his hooves, shake his rack, spread his scent around, and let his peers know this was his turf, these were his babes. Imagine the stepfamily variations in this crowd, I thought.

The four of us went on to see more animals, including huge tatanka, another elk, and herds of deer. We hiked in the woods and watched rainbow after rainbow come toward us across Yellowstone Lake while we had a cookout and climbed down to see the Grand Canyon of Yellowstone and Tower Falls. Sandy and I were impressed but not surprised that Cindy and John, serious workout devotees, were able to trot back up the 132 feet to the car from the gorge without even breathing hard. On the other side of the park, we watched Old Faithful shoot into the sky and toured the magnificent inn. Originally built for the Northern Pacific Railroad in 1903, it remains the largest log structure in the world. Behind two massive red doors with wrought-iron finishings in the Arts and Crafts style was the central atrium lobby. This glorious six-story vaulted space, with stone fireplaces, massive log supports, and wings of rooms spreading to the left and right, gives the traveler a feeling of solidity and civilization not at odds with nature.

We moved on to another emotional favorite, Grand Teton National Park. Less than an hour to the south, its landscape is radically different. Yellowstone's gently rolling grassy basin and range gives way to the sharp, craggy, snow-covered peaks of the Tetons. Named by a couple of Frenchmen for their favorite female body part, it's a magnificent area for mountain biking and touring. That evening we celebrated Cindy's birthday, although it was actually still three weeks away, at a place we had once fantasized into existence. On our first trip out west, we had imagined we would find a place where we could stay in our own log cabin. It would have a pot-belly stove in a cozy living room, and puffy down comforters and feather pillows on the rustic hand-hewn beds. Of course there would be steamy hot showers and endless supplies of drinks, invigorated by buckets of ice left discreetly at our door. The view of the mountains would be as breathtaking as the privacy. In the dining room, overlooking the lake, we'd have three divine meals a day. One of the remarkable things about the West is that dining in cowboy boots and jeans is not inconsistent with having a five-star meal served on white linen by an attentive professional staff. The one thing we forgot to include in our dream was that each cabin would be outfitted with horses and bikes. Clearly our western imaginations needed a little work. The four days we had spent at the Jenny Lake Lodge had been restorative and sybaritic. We wanted to share this place with Cindy. She was relaxed and happy as she contemplated turning twenty-eight. Her toughest decisions immediately at hand had to do with chocolate, caramel, or raspberry.

We enjoyed the chance to spend time with Cindy and get to know John better. Since they were leaving at dawn to catch a plane and we had an early morning date for Susie to have a tune-up, we said our good-byes that night. Perhaps we were building this family's history a little belatedly, but I felt good we were doing it.

18

The Fortune Garage

Fall came to the Tetons that night on a northern jet stream measuring nineteen degrees. It was the third week of September. We had propane heat, we had a down comforter, and we had each other. There is no way around nineteen degrees feeling cold when your walls are one-eighth-inch uninsulated plastic and the floor gets its warmth from your feet. I envied Cindy and John, who were on their way to balmy Arizona. We hustled out of that campsite as soon as we got the ice out of our water pipe/hose.

Driving south to Jackson, Wyoming, through the hole of land that makes up the valley, we were flanked by the sun rising on our left and the mountains turning gold with daylight and fall on our right. Just before the rise in the land, Jenny Lake held on to her misty blanket for warmth. Given the coughing and sputtering Susie had been doing in the passes and the new season we were obviously entering, we were heading to her check-up none too soon.

We found the Transue doctor's office tucked between a school, a moderate-income housing development, and the main road, in a huge Quonset building. Even inside with the doors closed, it was nippy on a morning like this. We were grateful when Paul, the owner, showed us to a small office near the back of the building, which had a small heater. He offered us coffee and invited us to use the office while he checked out what needed to be done on the Sue. The little room felt pleasantly warm and looked like an office anywhere. Outdoor pictures hung on the walls along with a couple of calendars. The desk was neither messy nor empty. Staples, paper clips, and a phone book, were within easy reach. I hadn't been in anyone's office in four months. It hadn't lost its familiarity.

Access to a phone line was complete bliss for eager e-mailers going through withdrawal. Despite Paul's invitation to make ourselves at home, we felt somewhat like trespassers. Scanning the wire that ran from the wall to the phone, we quickly and silently unsnapped it and clicked it into our computer. After locating the nearest electric outlet, we plugged in our cord and booted up. Working quickly and wordlessly, I thought we'd have made a good pair of spies in the make-believe mode of *Mission: Impossible.* Acknowledging "Sign on?" in the affirmative, we waited for the golden tones of modem meeting modem, and we were in. We had mail! Five notes brought us up to date on the lives of our friends. As we read the letters to each other and composed replies, we all but forgot our borrowed surroundings. Suddenly a tall, befuddled young man came bounding in through a second door to the office, which apparently led from a small parking area at the rear of the building. Grinning yet silent, he handed me a bill for $750, one-third of which, I noticed, was for antifreeze. They sure worked quick and big, I thought, wondering how many gallons of the stuff the Transue could possibly hold. Then I realized he had mistaken me for someone who actually belonged at this desk. This was not our bill—it was the garage's bill for a shipment of antifreeze, among other things. I declined to pay it, explaining I was a customer. Embarrassed, he actually shuffled away from me without turning around and backed out the door through which he had come in, muttering apologies. Sandy and I laughed, relieved we didn't need $250 worth of antifreeze after all, and finished writing letters.

E-mail sent and received, friends with 800 numbers called, too much coffee consumed, and Susie was still in the operating room. Nothing serious, just a bunch of dirty plugs and misguided wires. Rummaging around in our minds for something to do, we remembered that our friends Linda and Richard had a vacation home somewhere in Jackson. We tried calling them on the off chance they were in town and could meet for lunch, but there was no answer. As we were reaching the outer limits of our waiting tolerance, a woman came in through the back door. In her early to mid-thirties, she wore a purple dress with a cinched waist, cowboy boots, flowing hair, and a smile. Apparently it was not all that unusual for her to find strangers lounging in her office. She introduced herself as Mary, wife of the owner and proprietress of the desk. I never would have guessed this was the office of a dame. And I mean that in the best possible way. Mary was a pistol. We three hit it off right away. Questions and answers popped back and forth like tennis balls as we filled each other in on our recent histories. She understood our growing urge to reconfigure our lives. We found a kindred spirit. She was eager to hear what we were going to do; we were eager to hear what they had done in order to reach their decisions and how they spent their time now.

Mary and Paul had done "the big quit" about ten years earlier. Having lived and worked in Boulder, Colorado, for some while, they'd felt it was time to move on. Without a specific end goal in mind, they'd headed west, through Colorado to Wyoming and Nevada. Not finding what they wanted, though they still had no concrete idea what that was, they retrenched to Jackson. Starting without job prospects, family, or home to ground them, they took whatever work they could find. Paul first got a job as a mechanic in the place he now owned; Mary free-lanced in the business sector and helped Paul out as well. They spent as much time as they could outdoors and had most of the big boys' toys one could think of: a speed boat, motorcycles, snowmobiles, an MG convertible, a horse, and a dog. As if to seal our friendship, it turned out they shared our big passion for scuba diving. We were very impressed and energized by hearing how they had consciously carved out a life that balanced work with play.

It was a very short morning at the garage for Mary. While the car doctors worked their magic, we took her out to lunch. She drove us to a place called Bubba's—we probably wouldn't have noticed it passing through town on our own. It was a folksy place where everyone from the hostess to the waitress to the customers said hey to Mary as we walked to our booth at the rear. We grazed the big salad bar and had excellent barbecue. Listening to Mary's story and sharing our dreams with her didn't feel at all odd, even though we'd met her only a couple of hours earlier. Our New York guard was slipping and we didn't mind a bit. We compared notes about dive trips we'd taken, reefs we'd been to, and places we hoped to go. We spilled our dream guts, and she returned the same. She told us about the thrill of a bear visiting their house and how much fun they had at the lake in the summertime. Even though Jackson had grown a lot since they'd arrived and it was harder and harder to find a good house at a decent price, she encouraged us to look around. We built up a head of steam about Jackson. She should have worked for the Chamber of Commerce.

A few years back we had walked through Jackson on a rainy day. We hadn't thought much of it. We couldn't get past the fancy stores in the square. This time it really charmed us. We picked up the newly rejuvenated Sue from Paul. He urged us to run her up a hill, test her out. She drove better than ever, no knocking, no sputtering, no complaints. He had done a great job. We paid up, said thanks and good-bye, and headed for the real Chamber of Commerce, where we picked up all kinds of information. In the parking lot we spread all the brochures and fact sheets out on our dining-room table. The relocation packet had everything in it, from climate to culture. It looked like the Jackson area had a lot going for it culturally, something we'd determined we wanted. There was one brochure just listing all the galleries. A good sign for us, but was it "too cute"? Mary had mumbled something about it maybe being time for them to move on. Hmm. But it sure was a tidy-looking town, with charm, character, and history. A good brew, we thought. Asking each other questions about what we liked, what we wanted and needed, an answer started forming itself into a formless blob. Something the Starship *Enterprise* might have encountered in deep space. Could it support intelligent life?

Later that afternoon we saw several realtors. One was a snob, full of disdain for our expectation to find something wonderful in the, say, $250,000 area. The others were very helpful. We drove around to three "neighborhoods" to get a sense of where we might want to rent. (Buying was still too much of a commitment to contemplate.) We felt the first place, townhouse-type condos located inside in Teton Park, facing the mountains, might be right for us. It was startling that we were suddenly going about this as if . . . as if it were really happening. As if we were actually going to change our lives, not just talk about it. The reality nickel was slowly dropping. Looking at real estate was always fun, but this was *real* estate. How easy and hard it would be to reinvent ourselves, I thought.

In a somewhat trancelike state, we shopped, gassed up, and prepared to head south. I thought to try phoning our friend Richard again, this time at his office in Utah. He was there, jolly as ever, and slightly miffed that we hadn't called ahead to use their place. It was one of those light-bulb-over-your-head moments when he said, "Gee, you'd love our condo. It looks right over the Tetons." This would be too easy, I thought.

Funny, you never know when your fortune, or your future, will be changed along with the spark plugs in a garage.

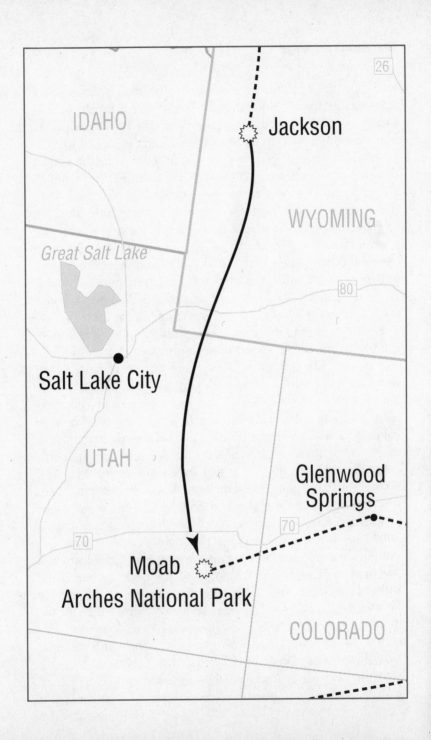

19

Mazel in Moab

We floated down through Wyoming, still titillated by the possibility and shocked by the reality of impending change. We talked our way through the whole state, stopping only for a sale on jeans and a bakery. After all these weeks of traveling light, the feeling that there was another purpose to our trip began to register. We tried to sort out our goals. Living to work to support our lifestyle was out. In practical terms it would be cheaper to live outside the New York City area, although the thought of leaving family and friends made me cringe. Unless we moved to Beverly Hills, we reasoned, we could probably ease our mortgage and tax burdens considerably. We wanted to be outside more. Though we didn't want to give up experiencing the change of seasons, I craved a sunnier winter. The place we would settle would have to be culturally alive and welcoming of newcomers, yet have an established sense of history. Instant 'villes had no appeal. It would be a place where we could work, though the details of what that work would be remained entirely fuzzy. Finally, since we were the ones making up this wish list, there would be plenty of good restaurants. The details and texture of what all that implied were unknown. The only thing we knew with clarity was that our lives were not going to be as they were. This was not just another two-week vacation wedged in between two slabs of work-as-we-knew-it. We didn't want life to be the same, yet different meant change: new, unknown, scary. Free-floating anxiety would replace stom-achaches brought on by familiar pressures. We continued to talk about it and agreed we were sick of the devil we knew. We were, almost positively, ready for a new devil. Sandy was more certain than I—perhaps because he had already made a major geo-graphic move, leaving Michigan for New York—that moving was a big part of the right answer. In the meantime we reached a new state, and the land around us grew redder than hell. We were in Utah.

At Dinosaur National Monument, surely the place where Mi-chael Crichton first imagined Jurassic Park, we hiked a red rock trail and saw a wall of prehistoric excavation in process. In si-lence we drove up and down the ten hairpin turns to reach the ten-thousand-foot summit of Flaming Gorge. Even the Sue was quiet in this surreal land. We surveyed the scene from our camp-ground at the midpoint as the sun retreated behind us. The horizontal stripes of color—reds, beiges, and tans—swept around the horseshoe of water far below. Each layer was a his-tory, an era, many lifetimes long. Naked mesas and parched buttes, once habitats of safety and refuge, were now islands in the sky, isolated and unreachable. With the colorful stripes of sand reminiscent of a fancy tank, I imagined the fish that once drifted in water that was now bone-dry desert air before me. One perfect skeleton, secreted in mud for centuries, then un-earthed, could cause legions of people to swoon. Our individual lives made every difference and none at all.

As extraterrestrial as the mineral springs at Yellowstone had been, as surreal as the waterless fish tank of Flaming Gorge was, the slickrock of Moab brought us to another constellation. We reveled in the sunshine. Glowing red rock slopes surrounded us. In the distance was the outdoor museum of perpetual disintegration, Arches National Park. Get it while you can, see it while it lasts. Pictured on so many maps, guidebooks, and other literature of the area, one almost feels a familiarity upon seeing the vaulting rocks. We had to snap to and remind ourselves that these were natural configurations, not manufactured by Ray Kroc or Walt Disney. Welcome to Moab, cycling capital of the USA. In the 1950s uranium was briefly mined here, causing chaos and calamity in this tiny town. Wealth beyond imagining was imagined, and a few people did get rich. That out-of-character, crazy time in the red desert is referred to by some as Mormons on a Bender. Moab.

Moab. The word almost forces you to whisper. *Moab.* You have to be very deliberate to get that final *b* out. *Moab.* It is mysterious. We drove into Arches National Park. The scenery was bizarre. Red sandstone formations, from 150-foot sheer cliffs, to pillars with delicately balanced rock heads, to arches in wild variety. Where it is ground by the wind, the rock becomes a fine powdery sand, almost right for coloring cheeks. Low sage-green brush and yellow and purple flowers completed the makeup kit. The sky was blindingly blue. Moab.

It was strange, and yet entirely appropriate, to spend the Jewish New Year in the desert. I seemed to have a significantly higher tolerance for this climate than Sandy; genetic imprinting, he said. I liked the sensation of baking, drying out, and absorbing the warmth from the earth. Especially after a summer in Alaska, there was nothing like Rosh Hashanah in Moab. Official synagogue worship never appealed to me, but I did feel as if I was the only lonely Jew in Utah.

The trail we took that day was toward Delicate Arch, the cover girl of all arches. From the observation point along the road, she was barely visible, though I held her image in my mind. Slim and curvaceous, she is a graceful athlete, her hands and feet firmly planted, stretching her bellybutton toward the sun. At three miles round trip, the trek was classified as difficult, though at first I could not see why. The dirt path was easy to follow, pounded daily by many feet. Shortly, however, across a small canyon formed by a stream that in other seasons may have had hope of floating something but now was merely a ditch, we saw little antlike things winding their way up the rock face. They were people, and we would be in their steps soon. Sandy forgot his hat and was dripping sweat. His Scottish ancestry was showing. I wore long sleeves against the sun and had my many-pocketed vest loaded with the accoutrements of touristdom: camera, film, tissues, lip balm, and water bottle. I felt serene, though I wished I didn't pant so much going uphill.

As we climbed the rock face, ordinary trail markers were abandoned. This was no place for signposts: there were no trees to which a ranger might nail a colored tag, and no one painted arrows on the rock. Someone had thought to indicate the way by placing little piles of stones every so often. It reminded me that when I was a child, we would leave stones on the graves of my grandparents. I never understood why. "So the family would know someone paid a call," my parents said. But we were the only family they had left. I thought it was so that God could see someone still cared, even after the war and Hitler.

We followed the line of sight to the next little pile, climbing steeper, breathing harder. Around a curve the ground to our left fell away. The trail became a ledge. Thankfully it sloped inward, allowing gravity to keep us safely tucked in. We finally reached the apex of the hike. Before us was a huge bowl carved from the rock. As if there had once been an amphitheater in the sky, various stone "seats" seemed comically molded to look like squishy hamburger buns. On the far rim stood the arch, the opening possibly sixty feet high. People braver than we were scrambled across the rim to walk under the curve of the rock. They looked like dancers on Mars, the red planet, to me. The noonday sun backlit their frolicking outlines. We looked toward the east and saw the earth spread out below us; way below, off in the distance, you could imagine the curve of the planet. This was better than going to temple, holier than being in a building. The synagogue was supposed to be the house of God, but surely there was some mistake. If that were true, then what was this? I felt a twinge of sadness at being the only Jew in Utah on New Year's Day.

Reluctantly, we began our return. We offered encouragement by way of smiling at the upward-bound walkers, who now loped slowly in the midday heat. Again I saw the little piles of rocks and wondered what I should be doing to sanctify this day, but the thought passed. It was good to sit down and drive on.

We picnicked briefly in a pullout by the side of the road and continued through the park. Clumps of gathered vehicles generally announced the best places for views, even before we could see the signage. We stopped several times to stare at the sights. After getting out to photograph yet another arch, we headed back toward the Sue. There was only one other car in the little lot, a rental. Its engine was running, and it was surrounded by four people, two couples it seemed. They were rummaging through the stingy desert earth, apparently looking for a tool with which to wedge open the door or window. It was a case of tourists outside, keys locked inside. Sandy and I went over to see if we could help. They nodded and pointed and yammered about which one was an idiot, who should shut up, and where they would find help in the desert. One fellow had managed to wedge his fingers into the driver's window, which he held slightly open with his considerable weight. The tips of his fingers were beginning to look like gumdrops from the pressure. Judging by the position of their electric window and door buttons, it seemed clear they needed some kind of long rod with which to reach in and stab something open. But the desert isn't a place where you can find fireplace pokers or ski poles lying around. Aha! It occurred to me we had a long aluminum rod with which we opened our awning. I ran to get it. Jamming it inside the window that the fellow was holding down—now with a bunched-up hankie to keep his fingers somewhat protected—I tried to "feel" my way toward the buttons.

"You see," said one of the wives, "the women always have practical ideas!"

Bad time to rub it in, I thought. The other guy dashed to the opposite window and began shouting directions to me.

"Over," he groaned.

"More under," he grunted.

"This way!" he demanded.

Two things became clear: (1) English was not his native language, and (2) if this was ever going to work, Sandy—calm, handy, and English-speaking—had to step in and direct me instead of this quasi-hysterical guy. He went around to the passenger door and faced me through the car windows. We focused on each other as if I were the player, he was my coach, and the game depended on this play.

Hunched forward, both hands on both knees, Sandy began. "Straight down. To the left. Your right. Down a little. Press."

Click, the door unlocked. Lots of smiles and thank-yous. One guy, now free to be casual and comedic, jokingly asked for our address, in case it happened again. As we walked back to the Sue, I called over my shoulder to him, "Where are you from?"

"Israel."

Not the only Jew in Utah after all, I thought, and decided to give him two of my six or so Hebrew words.

"*L'Shana Tovah,*" I said, wishing him happy New Year.

Shocked, he looked at me and then said something to his crowd and pointed to his head, as if he suddenly had an explanation for why I'd been able to figure out a way to help them.

"*Sechel,*" I said, pointing at my head and using up another precious word, this one meaning common sense.

"*Mazel*," he volleyed back, and smiled. "Luck. Ours for hav-ing met you."

They left, and we climbed into the Sue. I felt a strange con-nection to this place, those people, and the day. We were all lucky on a day like this. I thought it must be a good omen.

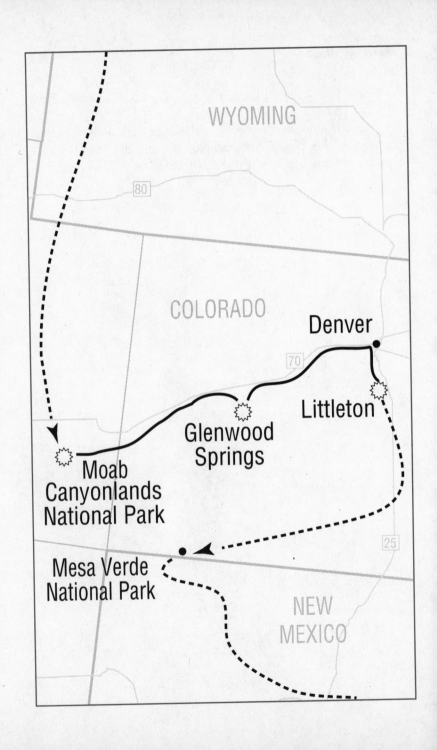

20

Gathering Marbles

We were still drifting through the possibilities of our dreams when we took a trip down the Colorado. Floating in the calm stream at this time of year was easy compared with fording the raging torrent it was in the spring or crossing the ocean it once had been. Red cliffs hovered above us, many dripping with black desert varnish. We relished the soothing day as an interlude between the emotional rigors of the past week and the sea of change ahead of us.

We spent a day in Canyonlands. Conveniently located just across the road from Arches, it presents a completely different terrain. Instead of leaving heaving shapes carved in space, this territory has deeply etched recesses. Where Arches takes your eyes skyward, Canyonlands takes them down. In Arches the smooth slickrock makes a damp impression. In Canyonlands layer after layer of eroding sandstone made me thirsty. Gouged deeply into the rocks below is the almost comically green Green River. This was surely the home of a devil we didn't know.

Nothing looked familiar, everything looked foreign. We spent the evening watching the sunset at Dead Horse Point, where we had a 360-degree view of the world. I had never seen the sun go down in the west and the darkness rise on the mountains to the east before. I felt like the center point of the seesaw in the solar system. We slept late the next day, exhausted by all our new discoveries.

*   *   *

Our unfettered days were waning. We had several dates to keep over the upcoming weeks. Our first stop would be in Glenwood Springs, Colorado, to visit Marianne and Timm. Marianne, and her brother Patrick Jr., were among the first people I remember on the planet. Our mothers met over strollers, and the couples became fast friends. Both women died young, but the men remained friends. Patrick and I were born a few days apart and spent many happy days tossing sand at each other in the playground. When Big Pat's work took them to Washington, D.C., we still spent holidays together. Usually we met midway along the Jersey shore, either in Atlantic City, then a crumbling resort town, or Wildwood, a quiet undiscovered beach area. Marianne, two and a half years younger than we were and a baby in our eyes, usually tagged along wherever Patrick and I went, even horseback riding on the beach. She still tries to make us feel guilty about the time we indifferently abandoned her under a pier, sobbing on a pony that refused to budge. We still laugh about the time we went on an Easter egg hunt and Patrick slipped on a wet rock, going into the creek in his Sunday best. And we remember each other's mothers. Since few people in my life now remember my mother, that connection seems even more important. Pat Sr. died a year ago and now there's just my dad. Though we hadn't lived in the same city for forty years, somehow we were friends.

*   *   *

Once upon a time it was easy to have and to be friends. You all lived in the same area, attended the same church or synagogue, and sometimes were even slightly related. (In some places I hear this got a bit out of hand, and over time people looked more and more alike and had fewer and fewer brains. But that's another story.)

Sandy and I are lucky. We have many good friends, some, like Marianne and Patrick, dating back to tiniest childhood. While we were on the road, physically removed from friends, in a funny way we became closer. Our e-mail correspondence was voluminous, particularly the responses to Sandy's (depending-on-the-electronic-gods) weekly journal transmissions. We loved getting mail. Visiting with family and friends, some of whom we hadn't seen in a while, had been on the agenda for this trip from the outset. Friends have always been terribly important to us. The prospect of moving to a new place and leaving them behind terrified me. Yet we had managed to maintain long-distance friendships with all these people we were now visiting. Perhaps it could be done. Then again, whispered the devil I didn't know, maybe not. What if people in other places were truly different, or thought I was? I didn't need to have the grade-school feeling of wanting to belong all over again. Once was more than enough, thank you. Is there life without friendships? I wondered.

As we traveled and spoke to people about their lives, from Alaska to Washington State, Montana, Colorado, Tennessee, and back toward home, an underlying motif of sadness drifted up through the conversations when we asked if they had many friends in their community. There were, of course, a few yesses, but the negative answer always drew my attention. Some shrugged off this lack, saying they preferred to spend time with their spouses and children. The absence of friends was clearly something I'd worried about, and hearing it reflected back at me as a reality made me uncomfortable and anxious to define, in my mind, the reasons for it, in order to be able to avoid it. Having friends was important. Having friends with whom one built a community was important. I wasn't looking for a commune or utopia. I was the last person anyone would even consider a "joiner." I just wanted to know there was a community I could be part of. If I wanted to. At my discretion. My choice. What a brat.

There seems to be this constant tug-of-war in the American nature and in me. Build a community. Be an individual. In New Hampshire the license plates read "Live free or die." An interesting though perhaps exaggerated generalization about the nature of individualism and how it relates to community. In the West, once known for its lawlessness, people still pride themselves on having their own space and being rulers of their own destiny. "Don't tread on me" still has real meaning and is given due respect. We came upon an example of how poorly Westerners take to being trod upon several years ago in Montana. We were late for a plane, and I desperately needed a bathroom. Sandy was driving a bit fast. A state trooper pulled us over, sidled up to the driver's side, and informed us we'd been doing twenty miles an hour over the limit, 75 in a 55 zone. Having no time to argue, we said, "Uh-huh," or something equally brilliant, hoping to just hurry up the torture. I crossed my legs tighter. Sandy showed him his license, the ticket was written up. At this point the trooper leaned down and said, "Do you think you have five dollars on you today?" I almost wet my pants. Was he asking for a loan? A bribe? Lunch money? Or was that the cost of the ticket? Five dollars? No points? For twenty over? "Sure," we said in unison in another fit of eloquence. We paid up and were history. It was later explained to us that when the federal government passed the fifty-five-miles-per-hour speed limit law, the state of Montana had never had a speed limit of any kind before. The theory was that the state wasn't about to monitor your every move. Montanans liked it that way. They weren't happy to be told by the feds what to do. So, in fact, they did very little about the speed limit other than to offer a "courtesy ticket" to speeders. That way they still got their highway money from the feds, but they didn't really get in anyone's face about how fast to drive on a road where you rarely saw another human. Pretty sensible, it seemed to me. Montana has since gone back to having no speed limit. Being unfettered by the feds is one facet of the "everyone for himself," "good fences make good neighbors" kind of attitude. Being an individual was fine by me, but I couldn't picture that the welcome wagon concept ever made it west of the Mississippi. I could be wrong, but that's how it felt. You could thrive, you could rot. It would be all the same to the guy on the next butte.

The men and women we spoke to reflected this attitude in their different ways when I asked them about friends. A fellow in Seattle, who had returned there after many years in the East, said he put his energies into work, and contrary to how it had been in New York, his work relationships didn't extend for him beyond that. A couple in their late forties, Dakotans by birth, who had raised three chilldren in one Montana city, were eagerly looking forward to moving to another town several hours away. They didn't give me any sense that they thought they'd be losing much. One woman, very outgoing by nature, had moved to Colorado three years earlier, when her husband's job had relocated him. They'd made no close friends in that time. A woman in a small town, whose husband had lived there before their marriage, said she felt she'd made acquaintances in the five years she'd lived there, but she felt no real closeness to anyone. That scared me. Where would we ever belong? Another item to add to the growing list of requirements: a place to belong.

*   *   *

We arrived in Glenwood Springs before our hosts got home from work. We let ourselves in with the key they had left for us. Sandy made a dive for the phone outlet to pick up e-mail, and I headed for the washer and dryer. Even though we'd never been there, we felt at ease. That's how it is when you visit friends, I thought. Marianne and Timm had a beautiful home facing a red mountain covered in fir trees. It was wonderful to visit with them, meet some of their friends, and play stick catch with their

dogs, black and brown Labs, Jessica and Keillor, who had perfected the hilarious art of joint fetch-and-retrieve. Together we
toured the extravagant town of Aspen, looked at an old family
album, soaked in the Glenwood hot springs (twice), and made a
series of memorable meals. It would not have been fun with
strangers. There are certain rules that dissolve when you are
with friends.

We crossed the state of Colorado in the north, hoping to
spend some time in Rocky Mountain National Park. As we
drove, cold weather caught up with us again, and snow turned
the landscape from full color to black and white. It was the first
of October. At 11,000 feet the weather turned raw. We decided
to head south.

Just before Denver the high mesa and mountains we'd been
on gave way to a huge expanse. We were looking down on the
geological beginnings of the plains and the Mile High City. We
stopped in to see Jody, a friend I'd worked with in New York.
Originally from the Midwest, she'd moved to Denver because of
her husband's work. The last time I saw her she had been very
pregnant. This time we met the adorable Peter, their ten-month-
old son. Dad was off on a business trip. The four of us caught up
over supper. We talked a lot about relocating, both the challenges and the up side. Jody had made an impressive start developing her own literary agency. Friendships, she said, were
slower in forming when you worked out of your home. An
interesting point to remember. It was a sweet visit, but short.
Needing to get some miles behind us, we headed off into the
night.

*   *   *

On the interstate we listened to a little CB jive. I remained
convinced it was always the same two guys, piped in for my
amusement. I could catch only every fourth or fifth word Nasal
Nose and Marble Mouth said, but hey, they never said much
anyway. Their conversations, such as they were, always seemed
to involve headlights of one sort or another. As we cruised along

in the darkness, I was glad we had seen our friends. Though we liked Glenwood, it hadn't sung to us. Denver's suburbs were like most others. No closer to knowing where we might land, but a bit wiser perhaps about what we were looking for, I fantasized about finding the right place and then tipping the earth just so, in order to have our friends roll in, like marbles.

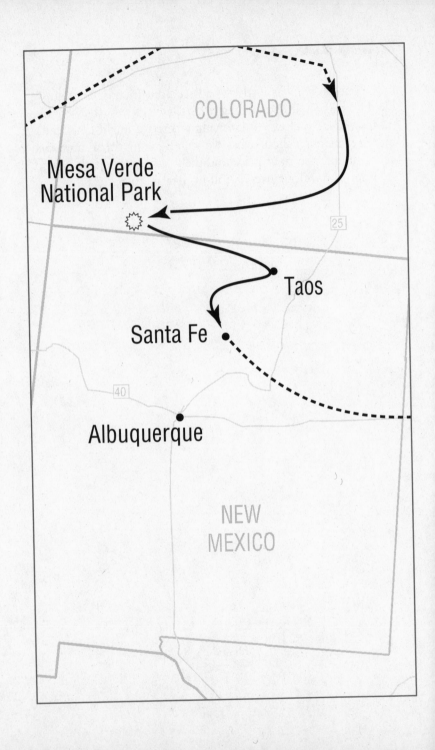

COLORADO

Mesa Verde
National Park

25

Taos

Santa Fe

40

Albuquerque

NEW
MEXICO

21

Ruin Junkies

We drove a backward "S" through Colorado, trying to reach all the places we'd heard of, falling in love with the one we hadn't, Mesa Verde. Unfortunately we couldn't move there, as the last residents had left more than six hundred years ago, but I'm sure we would have found friends among them. It was a magical, mystical place. An ideal place to spend the holiest day of the Jewish year, Yom Kippur. The way I've always understood it, eight days after the Jewish New Year, we're supposed to atone for our sins of the previous year and pray to be written into the Book of Life for the upcoming year. It is a day for fasting. As a child, when my mother was too sick and my father refused to participate, I would spend the day with cousins in their synagogue, located one flight above a men's clothing store. Theirs was a much more Orthodox shul than what I was used to. The congregation, segregated by sex, was largely immigrant and elderly. The services were somber. Old men rocked back and forth as they stood, draped in ancient prayer shawls, chanting in a language I could not understand. Heat rose from the street and the closely packed bodies. Stomachs grumbled, and breath was sour. Not even water was allowed. There were always fainters. A few strong young men seemed to be in charge of reviving procedures. I was supposed to concentrate on my sins, prepare to cast them off into the river, and pray to be written into the Book of Life. Instead I prayed that I could go home soon. I saw nothing religious in this torture, felt nothing spiritual in the air. I smelled sweat, bad breath, and my own impatience. When my mother died, my dad and I started a new tradition: Every year we had lunch together, just the two of us. This year I would miss that. Instead Sandy and I visited the Anasazi cliff dwellings.

The day was sunny, but raw and windy. Despite the fact that I had layered up in a T-shirt, a denim shirt, and then a heavy flannel shirt, I was still cold. We joined a school bus tour because there was so much to see in just one day. Our leader, Sam, proved to be knowledgeable and a real spark plug. A scrappy, energetic fellow, he was the last to comment on the increasingly cold weather, despite his short-sleeved shirt. Not a bad school bus driver, either. He probably had plenty of practice when he was track coach for the regional high school for thirty-one years. We met him at the campsite store that morning for a nine o'clock departure.

The setting was high mesa: nine fingers of land, from 7,000 to about 8,500 feet high, separated by deep canyons. The ancient ones who lived here had farmed the area since about the time of Christ. The name *Anasazi* is not their own word. It's a Hopi word, and some say it means "The Ancient Ones," while others say it means "Enemies of Our Ancestors." They are also referred to as "The Pueblo People" because of the way they lived. They abandoned their dwellings here around 1300. Like the Mayans, who created a vast culture, then disappeared mysteriously in Mexico, no one seems quite sure why they disappeared or dispersed. Though there are signs of drought, nothing definitive can be determined from them. Perhaps a war decimated these people, though unlike the Mayans, their culture was a gentle one, at peace for centuries. Had they been afflicted by plague, their remains should have been found en masse nearby. Some theorize they left their homes to follow a new religion. Around 1180 the people we call Anasazi—for we do not know what they called themselves—gave up their mesa-top homes and developed new ones in the natural sandstone caves all around the Four Corners area—the territory where Arizona, New Mexico, Colorado, and Utah now meet. These people continued to farm corn, beans, and squash, but they lived in "apartment houses" instead of ranch houses. Clearly, something had been wrong. Who would do such a thing voluntarily? our guide asked. We looked at each other.

The dwellings had been discovered by a couple of cowboys looking for errant cattle in December 1888. As one of them looked out across a canyon, instead of his livestock he saw a beige, multilevel sandstone structure with what appeared to be windows and towers. The walls were built of rocks, carefully shaped, bricklike, and joined by a mortar interspersed with small stones. The Anasazi were so much a part of their land that the cliff dwellings were at first invisible to us. From a distance only the large horizontal gash that was the cave entrance was apparent. As we got closer, details became clear: first shapes of square rooms and round rooms, then smaller openings that were windows, and finally the intricate brickwork. In places where they had been partially restored and structurally reinforced, we were able to climb in and out of these ancient homes. Approached by the original inhabitants from the mesas above via a series of finger- and toe-holds and ladders, we modern tourists were given idiot-proof access via Park Service paths. Peering into the windows, I saw several *mano y matates*. These horizontal mortar and pestles were primarily used to grind corn. Closing my eyes, I could imagine the back-and-forth motion required of the kneeling women who made the meal. It would have been hard work. These people also made jewelry, baskets, and pottery, combining artistry and elegance with necessity. The rooms in which they lived were roughly six by eight feet, just large enough for an individual or a couple to sleep or store goods. Central round chambers, known as kivas, were used perhaps for socialization or religious activities by each family. The kivas caught my attention. I wondered what had gone on in them. Were they festival or fasting chambers? Were they places of joy or terror? Did children sit and squirm while old men chanted and women fainted? Speculation among scholars has them as anything from the "dens" of their day, to the sites of secret rites open only to males. I kept thinking they looked (and the word sounded) like mikvahs, the Jewish ritual baths for women.

We came to Cliff Palace. Everything about the large multi-tiered structure looked solid and impressive. One of the rangers leading this part of the tour commented that no home like this would ever pass a contemporary building inspection, yet it was still standing a thousand years after it was first constructed. He went on to say there were hundreds, probably thousands, of them in this part of the world, only many of them remained hidden. Ironically, one way archaeologists find them is to wait for a natural disaster. A lightning fire, for instance, can reveal an overgrown site. These villages must have seemed mighty and impressive both to the inhabitants and to any newcomers. The clean lines of the structure were totally contemporary. Handsome color washes on exterior walls were still faintly visible. One interior wall displayed a bright sienna geometric design.

Yet the people were gone, leaving behind no message we can understand, nothing we can learn from about their demise. Only mystery and supposition are left to fuel our imaginations. How could a people at peace for so long, so wise about the land, so cultured, just vanish? What sins had they committed? I tried to atone for their unknown sins and mine and asked for time to tell at least one person that there once had been a people here who were just like us. Perhaps better.

* * *

Over the next several days we pointed the Sue this way and that to find more ruins. Like a good divining rod, she always came through. Chimney Rock, Aztec Ruins, and Salmon Ruins. We were becoming ruin junkies. Maybe it was easier to get lost in the past than to admit we were lost in the present, on our way to an uncertain future. Nevertheless, these were places of incredible beauty, usually with fabulous vistas, always with much mystery. The structures reflected quality craftsmanship, timeless design, and ingenious use of space. A thousand years from now, will people be saying the same thing about Trump Tower?

Once I went to an exhibit, "Art in the New World," at the Metropolitan Museum of Art in New York City. The exhibit of Native art was powerful. There was room after room of dramatic, earthy, honest art and craft, enjoyed by the entire populace in its time. Some pieces were comical, some had a frightening aspect, all were engaging. Then, as I walked through a doorway, *boom!* Here were the "discoverers" and their Church, with hideously gaudy gold and jewels that only a few folks had any access to. And scary paintings and statuary, bleeding, crying miserable souls. Good work, white man! I wonder what would have happened to Native culture if it could have remained "undiscovered."

In contrast to the ruins, the Native American towns we saw on reservation land all seemed to be ugly reflections of what our culture has done to take away the beauty of their lives. All over the West squalid towns, trailer village after trailer village, seemed to glare at us and say, "See, you stupid white people, this is what you wanted us to become—reflections of the worst of your culture. Now, instead of the beauty we once could have offered you, you will have to look at this ugliness forever."

High in the mountains we passed a lonesome ranch. On the crossbar where you expect to see the name of the place, a man had been hung in effigy. Around his neck a sign said "We'll do it the old way." I assumed these folks didn't require a newfangled alarm system either. Was it individualism or protecting the community? We didn't know. A little farther along we saw a huge herd of ghostly white cows. They marched in rows through the sage, heads down, as if they knew what was in store for them up ahead. There are at least a couple of ways to do everything.

In various villages around northern New Mexico, pueblo people still live the old way, in their own villages. San Juan, Santa Clara, San Ildefonso, near Santa Fe, are all populated by Native people who welcome outsiders to trade with them. They are great artisans, proud of their pottery, jewelry, and other crafts, and were delighted to take our money. Their tiniest blackware or redware pots cost $150 or more and some of their artisans had yet to hit puberty. They seemed to have been called to this work, perhaps as a way of capturing the past and making it present.

Our first overnight stop in New Mexico was in Taos, in the northeast. We were shocked and amused to find everything in the town built either in pueblo or adobe style—even the gas station and the supermarket. North of the town, in Taos Pueblo, a multistoried adobe village, several hundred Native residents live very much the way their ancestors did, without running water or electricity. In a way, they reminded me of the Amish, making do with temperamental and difficult-to-repair propane refrigerators in order to satisfy and honor "the old way." (It's a little like keeping kosher in the house. The house doesn't have to own up its sins at the end of the year, only people do. I guess all religions have their quirks.) Many old people live there in the half-abandoned emptiness. Some young families have chosen to move back, to pass the culture to their children, while continuing to create their art. The community is open to visitors (for a fee) with a camera (for another fee) or a videocamera (for a higher fee). Ha ha, you white guys!

The pueblo may not be paradise, but it certainly has integrity and heritage. The people I spoke to there (all shopkeepers and/ or artists) were proud of their work and their lives in the pueblo, in a way not apparent in the reservation hamlets of depression and alcoholism.

Maybe it was the desert color of the adobe village, or the

uneven streets, or the faces of the elders. Maybe it was the age-old activities of bread making, weaving, and grain grinding. Perhaps it was just the sensation of being transported to another time and place, yet one so universal it echoed with familiarity. But walking through Taos Pueblo I recognized something. I'd felt this way before, in another ancient city. A place where the walls are thick and high and the color of sand and the stones of the streets have been worn into little valleys by centuries of feet going to market, going to pray, going to the comfort of their homes. The place is Jerusalem, another ancient city, another pueblo. Walking through the dusty center of the Taos Pueblo, I thought about Jerusalem, how the matters of daily life went on and on, here and there. I passed a weaver's shop where rug makers worked, talked to an old man from whom I bought some beads. Women sold baked goods still warm from the outdoor ovens. Dogs barked, and children cried.

I felt reassured knowing that certain features of humanity remained the same over time and space. Everyone appeared to be happy in a warm tub of water, people everywhere enjoyed feasting and good food, and nearly every culture I could think of had spiritual beliefs of some sort. I recognized that it had been my own misconceptions, my fears, my narrow vision, that had made me see strangers we'd encountered on this trip, "them," as different from folks I knew back home, "us." Our trip was proving to me that Sandy and I had more in common with people we were meeting than I could have ever guessed. Even if I still did not know that exact nature of what we were going to do, it was still possible to feel nurtured, happy, and productive "out here." I tried to focus on the sense that even if we would not be going back to our old lives, in their usual places, life would continue in a recognizable form. The devil we didn't know lost its ferocity, at least for the moment. The sadness of change began to lift. I hoped—a secular form of praying—to be written into the Book of Life.

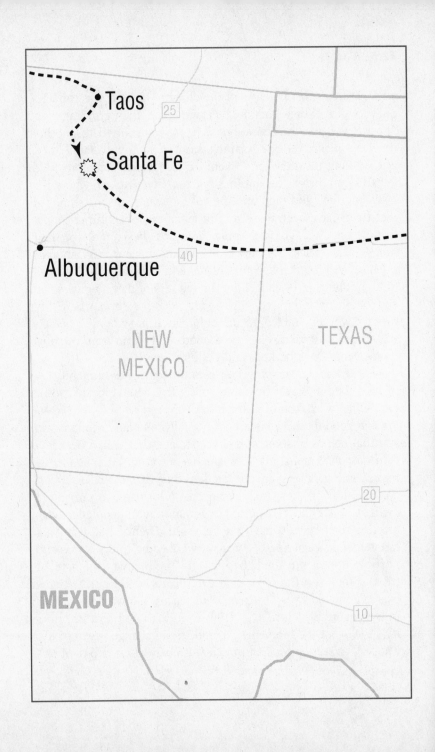

22

Full Moon
over Eldorado

We arrived in Santa Fe on the seventh of October and decided to take a vacation from moving and stay put for a week or so. When the Spanish came to what is now the southwestern United States, they had two things in mind: gold and God; cash and converts. Some say the two amounted to the same thing. While some made an attempt at holiness, others set out to find the fabled "cities of gold," Coronado foremost among them. He'd heard about the fabulous El Dorado. He never got there. Still, several hundred years later, with that same wishful thought in mind, a modern-day

Coronado had made it easy for us to get to Eldorado. All we needed to do was take I-25N to 285S and turn right. Our friends Bob and Shirley had been kind enough to let us use their vacation home. Bob and Shirley lived in Eldorado at Santa Fe. It said so on the adobe entrance to their subdivision. Unfortunately, due to occupational pressures, they couldn't join us. We had the house to ourselves.

It was a three-bedroom adobe with fabulous views of the mountains, deluxe bathrooms, phone lines, a television, a stereo, and a washer-dryer. Everything campers dream about. Naturally we e-mailed like crazy, laundered, lounged about, and took long Jacuzzis. It was amazing how quickly we moved in on the place and felt at home. Still, we wanted to sleep in the Transue, in our own bed. Altogether, it was heavenly. We were perfectly set up for a little R and R, with one exception. After doing it for one day, we realized that driving and parking the Sue in this city was not ideal. To be able to maneuver easily in and around town, we needed to rent a car. After all those months of sitting high up in those thronelike airline chairs in the RV, being in a compact car felt soooo low to the ground, it was frightening. As we drove out of the rental lot, we both reflexively leaned way back in our seats, away from the windshield. It was pretty comical. I dubbed our car the Roadlicker.

After all those months on the road, we needed a rest. Driving a thousand or more miles each week, making and breaking camp each day, squeezing in as many sights as possible all took their toll. Imagine the stress, dear reader. Imagine the strain. The life of a traveler can be rough. But being a tourist is another matter. As tourists we were free to sleep late, eat out, and keep no schedule at all. We became lollygaggers at large. It was not a difficult transition. The early fall weather was perfectly clear, pleasantly warm, and totally conducive to touring. On a walking tour we learned that Santa Fe had been an Indian settlement since around the first millennium, then became a Spanish outpost in 1602 and an American state capital in 1846. All the buildings in town had been restored earlier in this century in either the Pueblo Revival or Territorial style, creating a sense of age. The visual continuity drew a seamless connection with the colors of the landscape. Native artisans sold their work in the shade outside the Palace of the Governors. We had drinks in an outdoor garden in the middle of the afternoon and ate a late lunch on a second-floor patio. New Mexican food: spicy, salty, slightly greasy, a little bit naughty. All my favorite tastes. It was the beginning of a very good week.

The light in Santa Fe was something I'd heard discussed and described many times. It is said that, because of the altitude of 7,000 feet and the lack of humidity to hold particles down, the air is clearer here than anywhere else. Artists come here to try and capture scenes drenched in that uncompromising light. I knew about Georgia O'Keeffe and her sunbaked skulls. I expected parched, bleached colors and dusty barren land. What surprised me was the fields of canary yellow and lavender blooms, mountains covered with deep green pinions and golden ash, sunsets glowing magenta and purple. The desert shades were far more vivid than either of us had imagined. As we drove through the canyons, explored more ruins, and scoured the flea market, we felt enveloped in the warmth of the sun and the colors of nature.

We drove the Roadlicker along the scenic and ancient high road to Taos. The land undulated beneath our wheels, up and down, left and right, making us feel like cartoon characters. We were amazed at the number of bookstores in Taos, a tiny town of only five thousand people. At Bandelier National Monument we walked through history in Frijoles Canyon (Bean Valley would sound dopey) and gazed at more Anasazi condo vacancies. The adobe walls blended into the cliffs. Sunshine baked through the fall foliage and gave off a sweet aroma. Roadlicking back toward Santa Fe along the Rio Grande, we bought garlands of dried red chili peppers, ristras, to give to friends. At the pueblos Native potters invited us into their homes. Blackware, the natural coloring that came from dung smoke during firing, was a specialty of Santa Clara Pueblo. At San Ildefonso we saw redware. At San

Juan I bought a painting of a pueblo on a wooden bolo in the shape of a keyhole. It was thickly varnished with a tiny raised dot of a sun. I liked the way it felt. Going back into town was like time-traveling fast forward. Strolling in and out of fancy shops and galleries on Canyon Road, ordering food from menus, and paying with a slim plastic card suddenly seemed odd. But we felt good, very happy to have the mix of past and present, loving the sun and the climate.

At the end of the week we found ourselves at the Chamber of Commerce, loading up on another relocation packet and asking about realtors. Three were recommended. One was on vacation; one was glued to her phone and couldn't be bothered with walk-ins; and the third was John Grover, a tall, slim, patrician-looking gent. We explained our situation to him, as best we understood it. He broke into a smile and said, "Oh, have I been there!" Eighteen years earlier he and his wife, Joel, had left Boston and driven fourteen thousand miles in search of their next home. They ran out of gas and money in Santa Fe and had been there ever since. We gathered they'd done well together in the real estate boom. Like Mary in Jackson, John could easily have been head cheerleader for the Chamber of Commerce. He absolutely adored his adopted home. We drove around together (in his much larger car) to various parts of town and all kinds of properties, including one made from hay bales. We were all amused by the slightly off-kilter effect. The walls were skewed a little this way and that, as in a funhouse. John called Joel, and the four of us had lunch, talking as if we'd known each other forever. It felt as if another instant kinship were brewing. We must have been sending off new, revised vibes. Joel was at least as enthused about her town as John was. Did we know about the outdoor opera? There were excellent museums, world-class galleries, community theaters, several bookshops, plenty of movies, and many many great restaurants. There was skiing in winter, though it was usually sunny, and in the spring there were flowers everywhere. We were swooning. Could this all be true? Why were there only seventy thousand people here and not seven million? We absorbed what we could and went home to sleep on the rest.

In Eldorado we watched the full moon rise. It was the moon after harvest. The days and nights had begun their power shift. The equinox had passed, summer was officially over. Gardeners and farmers were taking in the fruits of their labors from the fields as they prepared for the next phase of living until spring. Since ancient times these annual cycles of nature have been observed and honored by humans. Every culture through time celebrated a harvest feast, just as winter solstice festivals have signified the reversal of the march of darkness since time immemorial. While the arrival of spring or summer may have seemed full of good cheer and frolic, the arrival of fall, the equinox, was serious business. Long before Wall Street earnings reports, life was measured in quarters: summer solstice/fall equinox/winter solstice/spring equinox. Payments were due to the gods if you wanted to get through to the next period. My response was an inexplicable urge to make soup, to put on a big kettle to boil and hunker down. I hated the fall, the darkness, the season of death. I would have happily hibernated. As I wondered about the larger cycle of life ahead of us and how we would accommodate to it, I felt the inexorable pull toward the rhythms of the universe.

Listening to the sounds outside, I gathered that coyotes did howl at the full moon. Humans generally have found the howling romantic or crazy-making or both. Perhaps it was the full moon or the changing of the season. Possibly it was a result of staying put in the same spot for one whole week. It felt like time to take stock. It felt like time to worship what sunshine we had left. It felt like time to haul in all our stuff and get ready for the onslaught of darkness and cold. It felt like time to nest. It felt good here, peaceful and light. Was this home, or was I just another lunatic? I wanted to dig in, make food for the coming season. Could this be the place of our future?

23

Pandora's Box

Casting a longing look over our shoulders, we got back in the Sue and headed directly east. We needed to keep dates, make time. We promised we'd be in Vermont for our family's traditional Thanksgiving celebration. Our plan was to be home by early November, an arrangement partly made of necessity since, as we went north, many of the campgrounds would close after the thirty-first of October. It was already the sixteenth. And, too, we had a gnawing sense that we needed to "make plans for the future," "get real," "get on with life." South of Santa Fe the land quickly turned to true desert. By the Texas Panhandle it was parched, dusty, and desolate. Nothing appeared cultivated. We saw no livestock. It looked like an alien land. Not gonna live here, I thought. The wind kicked up, making it difficult to hold the Sue on the road. Big and empty, she was like a road sail. A prairie schooner. The highlight of that day's drive was a no-fat soft yogurt, vanilla, in a cup, from a lonely Stuckey's. It was grainy and tasted bitter. We drove some more. It took concentration to hold steady. Without water or trees around, it was impossible to anticipate the wind. Keeping a firm grip on the wheel, we took turns driving. After 430 miles, we stopped at Elk City, Oklahoma. We ate, we slept. In the morning we moved on. We were nearly at sea level. Had we imagined Santa Fe?

In the daylight Oklahoma was quite pretty, radically different from the Texas we'd been through: large deciduous trees, mostly still green, and trimmed fields of red earth that had been harvested and plowed. Gentle hills went off on either side of the highway. The scenery began to have a familiar ring to it. The wind was down, and we were able to relax a little. Our heading was still due east along I-40. Most of this interstate overtook what had been the fabled Route 66. There was still a real romance in this part of the country about that old road. Collectibles were everywhere, including, now, on my husband's back. At the Santa Fe flea market he'd bought a denim jacket with a brocaded Route 66 design. Whenever we got out of the Sue, at a campground, gas station, rest area, people would ask him where he got it, give him a thumbs up, or just smile as if he were a member of their club. It amazed us. I tried translating this to the Northeast. Would anyone care if I wore an Albany Post Road T-shirt? How about a Mass Pike jacket? Even though it ran from Maine to Florida, I didn't think there were any Route 1 devotees or I-95 fan clubs. Route 66 had magic.

By lunchtime, we were in need of a little magic. Food magic. Consulting Jane and Michael Stern's *Roadfood*, we located Van's Pig Stand in Shawnee, Oklahoma. This wonderful book tipped us off to places with local color and regional tastes. Van's served up baskets of smoky ribs, piles of fries, slabs of Texas toast, and giant sodas to shoot it all down the hatch with. It was the perfect prequel, we thought, to spending the night at the home of the woman who had written the cookbook called *So Fat, Low Fat, No Fat*. Her name is Betty, and I'd met her on the phone a couple of years earlier. A local bookseller had tipped me off to the fact that this woman, as he breathlessly referred to her, had lost all this weight and self-published a low-fat cookbook and was selling it out of the trunk of her car. Every time he had her in his store to do a demonstration and signing, she sold books like, well, like hotcakes. Breathe, breathe. Get hold of her, he implored me, and publish her nationally. I did, we did, and her book sold hundreds of thousands of copies by the time I left my job. I had met her husband, Bob, briefly when they were in New York while Betty appeared on one of the national morning shows. She said she thought she had died and gone to heaven and had only one other goal in life: to be on QVC. Betty and Bob were the only people I knew who, when I told them we were going off to live in an RV for months, said "great" as if they really meant it. I thought Sandy would like them both, though I wondered what we would have for dinner.

Gore, Oklahoma, at the junction of OK-100 and OK-10, is about as far from midtown Manhattan as one can get. When I asked for directions to her house, Betty said it was the big white one on the left. It was that simple. As we drove up, she came out through a side door, still svelte in her shorts, to welcome us. Built ten years earlier but designed with care to look like a Victorian-era farmhouse, the big white house in the middle of the huge green field was a place out of time. Comfortable and comforting, it felt like a place I'd been to in my dreams of Americana. There was a kitchen and a summer kitchen, together supplying her with three ovens and twelve burners on which to test her low-fat compositions. She reminded us that these were the very same appliances that had helped her gain those sixty-six pounds over the years. A tinned ceiling in the living room, a doll collection in the attic, a cellar full of food put by. I had to remind myself that it was nearly the end of the twentieth century. You could feel a pleasant slowness, even in the breeze that puffed up the white gauzy curtains.

After the house tour, Betty said we were going to meet Bob and spend the night up at their summer place at Tenkiller Lake. More driving, I thought. "It's just up the road," she assured me. These Oklahomans do not lie—it was about ten miles away. Not only was it close by, their house was adjacent to a beautiful RV campground that faced the water. We situated the Sue and drove up the hill with Betty to her retreat. Her project of the summer had been to build on a huge deck. Though there was still some finish work to be done, the deck ran the fifty-foot length of the house. She called it a "helluva deck," and it surely was. The four of us spent the afternoon there, overlooking the lake, sipping cool drinks in the autumn sunlight. We talked about work and houses, kids and parents. We laughed at our preconceived notions of each other's lives. Again we noticed it was nice being with another couple who liked being with each other. Over a fine filet mignon dinner, we talked about life changes—those that had overtaken us and those that we were still shaping. They asked us, smiling as if they knew in advance what the answer would be, if we would consider moving to Gore. We said no, just as we would have six months earlier. Only now I was less sure of why I felt that way. A Pandora's box of possibilities had been opened and lay at our feet. How long would we chew over the contents before we swallowed? If the world was our oyster, why was I suddenly gagging? I was clearly coming down with a case of high panic. Time to drive, she said.

* * *

What we needed, as my uncle Howard used to say, was a nice *schvitz*. Sweat lodge, *schvitz*, steambath. Egg roll, blintz, manicotti. Same thing. It had been too long since we'd had a hot tub. We headed straight for the mother of all spas, the grand dame of good soaks, the city of steam, Hot Springs, Arkansas. A half-day drive from Gore, the city had the odd distinction of being, in part, in a national park. Rather than the natural redwood or plastic outdoor tubs we were used to, however, this was an indoor affair. The spring side of town was genteel and elegant, a reminiscence of the early part of the century, when ladies and gentlemen had come to "take the cure" for several weeks at a time. There was something soothing in just looking at the time capsule of houses along Bathhouse Row. Designed in distinctly different styles from Federal to art deco, they had once vied for business and offered special baths supposedly good for a particular ailment. Those claims were no longer made. We chose the Buckstaff Baths because they were open. The building looked like a pre–World War I men's club, substantial but friendly, with striped awnings and wooden rockers on a long porch. It was a reassuring kind of edifice. I felt my life taking shape just by looking at it. Inside, decades of organized pleasure oozed from the walls. Women went to the left, men to the right to change in white-tiled chambers. Wrapped in a sheet, toga style, by an attendant, I proceeded through the circuit. First, a nice long soak in a porcelain tub, then a steam in one of those stainless-steel contraptions that left my head sticking out of a hole. Sweating has never been one of my great strengths, I just turn red. Upon my release, I was led to a table where hot towels would be applied to the area of my choice: I chose my back. Next, re-togaed, I was led to what they called a needle shower, which squirted me all around at every level with a fine hard spray. Draped once more, I was left, reclining, to wait for my masseuse. A thirty-minute rub, and I was directed to another room and the cooling tables, the regular showers, and my clothes. My mental particles rearranged by the powers of water and Norma, the masseuse, I found my husband a-rockin' on the porch. He looked clean, buffed, and happy.

We began to inch our way east and north. This was the last leg. We could have turned around at any point, but we'd said we'd be home by Thanksgiving, and October was almost over. Our visits were coming closer together now—we had four coming up in a row. We were losing something, I wasn't sure what. I had a feeling something was gaining on us. We continued on through the flat land of eastern Arkansas, making for the mighty Mississippi River.

* * *

It was impossible to drive into Memphis without hearing Paul Simon singing in my head about bouncing into Graceland.

Rather than hear me do it a cappella, Sandy popped in the tape and let Paul do it. We were going there to meet up with sister Helen, who was flying down for the weekend from Michigan. High school class of '56 and every inch a bobby soxer/poodle skirt gal, she wanted to pay homage to the King. And to bring back some appropriate doodads for the Elvis shrine she had created at the elementary school where she was principal. I was sure Thompson Elementary had the highest density of six- and seven-year-olds in the nation who could recite all the lyrics to "Love Me Tender."

I was not against going to Memphis, but I was not really looking forward to it either. After all our time in nature, I feared it was going to burst the bubble. I was sure I wasn't ready for a city of one million people. Then I worried that we wouldn't be able to find enough for Helen to do. Given all the energy she had, I didn't know if one dead singer's house could keep her amused for a whole weekend. Next, I was a little skittish about being in the South. Weird things happened in the South. Especially to Yankees. Especially since the recent unpleasantness, if you know what I mean, sugar. Finally, I'll admit, I always thought Elvis had named the place for his mom, and I thought that was a bit peculiar. I'd heard they'd been very tight. Turned out it was called Graceland after the original owner's wife's aunt. Elvis's mom was Gladys. That's how bad rumors start. Still, for some combination of those reasons, I was a bit uneasy.

Sure enough, as soon as Helen came through the gate at the airport, she announced she was changing her ticket home to an earlier flight. She'd checked it out from the air and was sure there wasn't much to fuel her fire in this town. She'd go home early Sunday, get in a session of Jazzercises, and do some yard work. Welcome to Memphis. Our Graceland tour tickets were for the next day. While we waited, we were advised, the main events in Memphis were the following: go downtown to the Peabody Hotel at five P.M. and watch the ducks parade out of the lobby fountain and into the elevator for their nightly ascent. Eat lamb ribs at the Rendezvous. Listen to music on Beale Street. The riblets were the highlight of the evening.

In the middle of an endless strip of car dealerships and Shoney's restaurants is the former home of the greatest, most successful entertainer of all time. There was an otherworldliness to visiting Graceland (pronounced in one fluid verbal motion as *Grace*lend). As our ticket time and tour number were called, we were given an audiotape and headset, which was to be our personal guide. What we were about to see and where we would go was all carefully and cheerfully narrated by Priscilla Presley, among others. Of course there was appropriate background music at all times. We pilgrims (many gray-haired and well into their sixties or better) quietly boarded small buses at the main tourist entrance on the south side of Elvis Presley Boulevard— the true boulevard of broken dreams for so many who had obsessed over the King in their youth. The buses slowly and ceremoniously crossed the street, letting us off in front of the mansion.

It's a simple southern-style home: stone and wood trim, pillared and porticoed, on 13.8 lovely acres. Originally built in the 1930s by a doctor, Elvis had bought it in 1957, when he was twenty-two, for $100,000. Several outbuildings were added to suit his obsession du jour—a racquetball court, a shooting range, and the like. The interior was very 1970s, from a white trash perspective. It didn't wear well over time. The jungle room with puke green shag carpeting was especially scenic. We toured the home (downstairs only, bedrooms not included), racquetball building, trophy room, and meditation/burial area. All the while each of us was in our own private taped Idaho. Everyone was absorbed in thought and memory: fifteen again and seeing Him for the first time; fortysomething and learning of His death; trying to come to grips with the fact that, had He lived, He'd be in His sixties now. The endless stream of visitors were subdued. On the tape Priscilla insisted repeatedly how much laughing and joking had gone on in this room and that. Every woman listening must have thought the same thing I did: If things were so darn wonderful, why did he always have all those guys, his Memphis Mafia, around him? No wonder the marriage faltered. And yet here was this boy—and he had been a boy when fame found him—making a home for his family and friends. For twenty years he always came back to this place.

One of the outbuildings became an office for his father: a simple affair of desks, phones, and beige metal filing cabinets. An invisible VCR played an endless loop of Elvis on an old TV. We stood and watched as the King sat in that very room, fresh from serving with the U.S. Army in Germany. He was still very handsome, and in conversation (as opposed to while singing or in still photos), his demeanor was naturally sexy and engaging. Out of uniform and relaxed, this southerner who had just given service to his country politely answered the questions of the media, who were also still kind of shy and polite in those days. They asked him, but did not press, about a rumored romance abroad. He actually squirmed in his chair, cast his eyes up and down a few times, and protected the innocence and the privacy of the girl who would one day be his wife. Watching that brief tape, I caught what I'd never noticed before but what millions had gathered at the time, I'm sure—here was a true American naif, his face sliding all over itself and practically blushing on that old black and white screen. It was a painful reminder of an innocence that he, and all of us, would shortly lose forever.

Past the grazing horses and the gravesite, we returned our automated stream of preprogrammed consciousness to one of the guides (who never guided) and boarded the bus back to the other side of the street. The one-minute ride served as a decompression time between zones. If we had just been to the shrine, to Mecca, the south side was the commercial side of the street. Here we saw the King's cars, motorcycles, planes, and other less holy objects. It seemed each area was separated from the next by a gift shop. I thought of it as the Shop 'n' Weep approach. Or the Cry 'n' Buy. Sob at the pink cadillac, buy a miniature pink cadillac. Weep at his once-young face, take home a poster. Helen bought enough stuff for an entire school full of kids.

I admit I've never understood the "Elvis" thing. I grew up a few years too late, and he was not a serious contender for my rock and roll affections. But something caught me by surprise about the simplicity of it all and about the irony of Lisa Marie marrying the anything but simple Michael J. (I felt relieved on his behalf when their divorce was announced.) As I left Graceland, I felt a bit subdued, as if I'd found something and lost it all at once. Perhaps everyone has their own Pandora's box, and how life turns out depends on what you do with the contents. Elvis's was full of fame. Ours was filling up with ideas.

24

Tony Bennett
and Me

Except for Elvis, we all survived our trip to Graceland. Helen went back to Michigan, the ducks went back to work at the Peabody, and we drove on. I hadn't thought about it when we planned this part of our trip, but we were really becoming change detectives. We sought out people who had been down the road of relocation, dislocation, and upheaval ahead of us. Our friends in Nashville, Jo and Ira, had moved there a year or so earlier. Since Ira was in the music business, it had been only a matter of time before he landed there. Jo, an ace copywriter and marketing executive, had decided to seize the opportunity and leave the corporation. Still in a transitional phase, she was trying her hand at a variety of things, seeing which fit best. I admired her attitude. She had no preconceived idea about how this portion of her life was going to turn out. One thing was clear: She did not miss our mutual corporate past

either. It was wonderful to catch up with the world's best
e-mailer face to face. We ate well, toured well, and felt good
being together. Yet somehow the clock in our heads was ticking.
We didn't want to go home, but our self-imposed leash was
tightening.

Somewhere in Kentucky it started raining. As a consolation
prize, we found our cheapest gas of the trip: 89.9 for regular.
Lunchtime, and no bakeries in sight. While Sandy drove, I
nuked frozen New York bagels that had 14,500 miles on them
and were still pretty tasty. Next stop, Cincinnati, and the driveway of friends, Ed and Marci. They too had moved within the
last year. He'd bought a business he was struggling with, and
she was trying to develop her psychology practice. Not an
easy thing to do in the current health reform climate. They
were thrilled to have visitors from home. She knocked herself out and cooked a fancy French meal. Sandy weeded out the
brussels sprouts from the carrots. Marci pretended not to notice. That's a real friend. Next morning we were on our way
again.

In West Virginia the fall colors were nearly peaking. The rolling hills, with occasional barn, horse, or paddock, reminded
me of the American primitive scenery on our bathroom wall-
paper. Art is Life. Life is Art. As we came into the home stretch,
our pace picked up. Lingering was impossible. We visited the
Scotts, Sandy's family on his mother's side. Aunt Helen was
always a favorite of mine. My mother-in-law's younger, wilder
sister, Helen had been married and divorced twice, lived in
several states, taught college-level English, and raised two boys.
I got the impression she'd raised a little hell in her day too. We
hadn't seen her in three years; now we visited her in the home
where she was recovering from surgery. Cousin Tom, a physician, warned us that a stroke the year before had left its mark.
We peered into the dining room, where a sea of white heads
were bobbing over their early bird specials. I knew things

were fine when they rolled Aunt Helen out to us in a wheel-chair, dressed in chic black slacks and black and white sweater, complete with earrings, and lipstick on her round cherubic face. We had been sending her hard copies of our e-mail, and she remembered more about our trip than we did. She demanded we roll her outside so she could get a look at the Sue.

"You kids," she said, smiling. "I think it's just great what you've done. You kids."

Not many people called us kids anymore, and the encouragement was right on time. I needed a little emotional reinforcement just then. One thing I felt was certain about Aunt Helen's future—she wouldn't be hanging around with those old birds long.

That night we had supper at the country club with Tom and his wife, Jean. Still a practicing orthopedist, Tom had recently become the first Republican state senator since anyone could remember. Quite a transition, I thought. He liked politics and loved meeting people and doing the social thing. Jean, a very pretty brunette, smiled as if to humor him and said, "Why you know, you're not officially dead in this town until Tom Scott's been down to the funeral home to shake a few hands."

Maybe politics and doctoring aren't that far apart. Both are about fixing things, making people feel better. It was a good visit.

* * *

After being sociable almost continuously for a week, a night in the woods alone felt incredibly liberating. We had become accustomed to being quiet, having time to read and time to think, often referred to back home as "doing nothing." The only acceptable way, I remembered, to "do nothing" was to take up meditation. Then you could do nothing but actually be meditating so it was regarded as okay. I thought meditating was fine, but it wasn't doing nothing. That was something else again. Weird.

Steaming up the windows of the Sue, water boiled for pasta. In the hills of northern West Virginia, we sat side by side on our sofa and hugged, mentally bracing for reentry into the world. Our rolling nest had never felt cozier. We ate dinner by candlelight while heavy rain and strong winds brought leaves down around us by the bushel. We continued in our Greta Garbo mode, wanting to be alone. Were we heading in the wrong direction? Before we went to sleep, we changed our watches back to Eastern Standard Time. By any measure, a phase was coming to an end.

The last element of this trip that we had planned before leaving home was a visit to Fallingwater, the Frank Lloyd Wright–designed home of a Mr. and Mrs. Kaufman, in southwestern Pennsylvania. It was pleasantly distracting to be tourists for a day. The remarkable cantilevered house leans out over a stream and, in effect, becomes part of it. Local stone and Wright's audacious use of seamless glass corners give the impression that there is no difference between inside and outside. It is a magnificent achievement to look at. But it must be a miserably damp and cramped home to live in. Wright was five foot eight, and damn anyone who was taller, he designed houses that suited him. We strolled around the property, now 4,600 acres owned by the Nature Conservancy, and enjoyed the colors.

As we headed east through Pennsylvania, the sun refused to break through the gray clouds. Everything looked to be made of metal: steel sky, copper leaves, iron road. Around four o'clock a little blue crack appeared, allowing a faintly yellow, weak sunlight through, moments before darkness fell. The scent of wood smoke from houses nearby cheered me a little, but not much. It was much too soon to go home. Just as the beginning of the trip reminded of youthful days at camp, now I remembered the feeling of dislocation going home. I was also jolted by the first night of the new time. It was dark much too early. The first night of winter time is my least favorite night of the year. I hate the theft of that hour of daylight, the sudden blackout, and the implication, the threat that it will only get worse. This year it was doubly difficult because it turned out to be our last night on the road. This was death-of-the-year time, the time of year when my mother had died, my aunts had died, my cousin had died, and all life died. I hate this time of year, and especially this artificially truncated day.

Our last night camping we found a place miles off the highway, which was good since we were getting dangerously close to "civilization" or, at least, suburbs. It was pitch dark when we arrived, and the office was closed. Without regard for views, we hooked up in the first site and decided to take showers before it got too cold. It would be good to get under the hot spray. I gathered up the necessary equipment and made a dash for the shower house. Pushing open the heavy metal door, I saw that the lights had been dimmed for the evening, creating a moody effect. I was alone in a room meant for a dozen or more women, with four toilets, three shower stalls, four sinks, and a baby changing table. Music played from speakers in the ceiling. The acoustics were grand. It was the voice of Tony Bennett. Rich and familiar, reassuring and effortless. It required nothing of me: the words were not important, just the calmness they evoked. There was a certain timelessness about it. It could have been 1995. It could have been 1955. In my mother's kitchen during that time before dinner, while we waited for Daddy to come home, the radio was always on. As I peeled off my layers of road clothes and walked under the hot stream of water, the words faded completely, leaving the comforting rhythm and reverberation. I shampooed twice, shaved my legs, and got ready for civilization. The music was still playing, the singer was still singing. Though some things in my life had changed, the earth was still beneath my feet, and I knew we were going to be okay, no matter which direction we headed next. Drying off enough to get into cozy flannel shirt, sweats, and slippers, I made a run through the chilly night for the Sue, that soothing voice still humming in my head. Maybe it wouldn't be such a bad fall this year after all, I thought. Thanks, Tony.

*   *   *

I was driving when we reached the last tollbooth. We'd both been quiet, trying to absorb the weight of the "real world." In front of us the majestic steel and glass skyline of Manhattan loomed. I handed the toll taker a ten-dollar bill and stared at the city, waiting for change. Abruptly, a huge voice echoed through the Sue. It had the purity and resonance of a baritone preaching in a cathedral.

"Pardon me, do you have any Grey Poupon in there?"

I jerked upright in my seat and stared at the toll taker, but his lips weren't moving.

"Who said that?" I stupidly asked Sandy.

"Your old pal, Marble Mouth. The CB is on." Of course. What a dummy. The clarity of the sound and my ability to understand the speaker were amazing.

"As a matter of fact, I do," I replied. There were dozens of truckers around us. Which one was he? I took my change from the attendant and eased away from the booth slowly.

Now I had a coach. "You're lookin' good, darlin'. Come ahead. I wish my old lady would drive when we're on vacation. Twenty-four seven, all I do is drive. Got any hot coffee in there?" he ventured.

"Sorry," I said, laughing with my new best friend, "kitchen's closed until dinner." Which one was he?

"Well, have a good one, honey. Take care."

"Ten-four. You too, buddy."

Sandy and I smiled at each other, then grinned, then laughed out loud. How nice a simple conversation with another person could be—especially when we finally understood what he was saying after 15,241 miles. Now he sounded as clear as Tony Bennett.

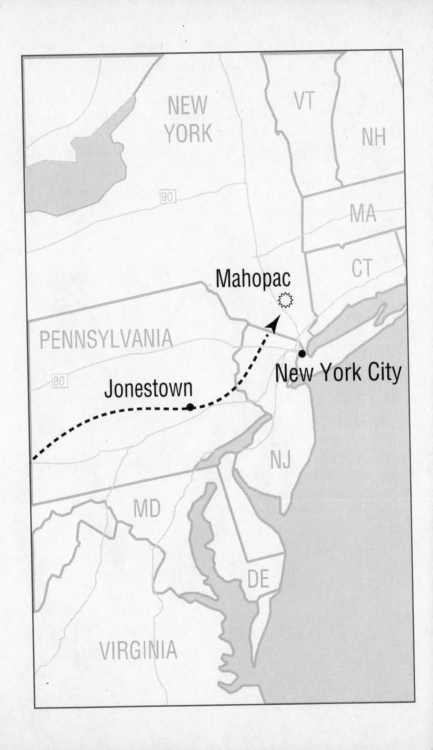

25

The Do/Be Ratio Calculation

<u>or</u>

Change Is Not a Dirty Word

We were home for the holidays. We had a cocktail party to welcome ourselves back, Thanksgiving in Vermont with the family, Christmas and New Year's with our regular troop of friends, a warm and fuzzy reunion with Pete and Norm. It was good to see and be seen, but now we had to prove we were more than just a novelty act. We had always felt the trip was supposed to be an interlude. Now what?

When the driving stopped, the planning started, but even the logistics of that process were not obvious to us. Although we had to care for a house and an apartment, we no longer had any reason to spend the work week in the city, the weekends in the country. We had no obligation to be anywhere at all. In fact, the disjointedness of going back and forth became apparent in a way to us that it never had been before. We came home to a schizoid life. A spacious house on a quiet lake, in a community where we had no roots. Outside, a few colorful leaves still gave off their scent of death in the watery sunlight. Around the apartment the city streets were humming with life and full of triple-parked cars. My favorite cardboard sign, propped in a window, said,

NO RADIO, NOTHING IN CAR, NOTHING IN TRUNK, THANK YOU.

Thank you for not smashing my windshield or stealing my car. That's my town.

I was confused. Home was where? We loved our house and had put ourselves and our souls into rebuilding and decorating it, but I now realized I felt no sense of place at all when we were there, outside our perimeter. Perhaps since we had always come there to collapse and recuperate after working seventy-five-hour weeks, I found myself immobile there. It seemed like no place at all, more like a rehab. In the city we had a tiny New York apartment, but the world outside was huge and beckoned. My adrenaline pumped like mad. Being in the city was like drinking a sextet of espressos. And whenever I was there, I loved it, but now I also noticed I felt a little like the Energizer bunny, banging a drum, going around in circles.

By any yardstick we had "made it" in New York, so according to the Chairman, Frank S., we could make it anywhere. But from what we had seen, I don't think there was anywhere else to make it that had rules I understood. What, exactly, would making it in Wyoming entail? This here was my game, *the* game, as far as I was concerned. That is, while I was playing the game. Game's over. Time's up. I had chosen to put myself out of play, and now what? I loved spending time on the road. No time or reason to think—just, literally, go with the flow. Get to the next stop, the next campground, meal, or mountain. Somehow, being stationary, all the little demons in my mind started to circulate, singing a low but demanding chorus of "Whaddaya gonna do, huh? Whaddaya gonna do, huh?"

Back in the swing of things, the net of the familiar, people began to lean on us about our intentions. Well-meaning friends, family, and former colleagues tossed job possibilities our way, forcing us to reconsider and recommit to our decision to build a new life, even if the particulars remained vague. We had learned to live outside the box we had previously put ourselves in and had felt expansive in a world without bounds. We learned to embrace the freedom outside those four walls where the pictures were always safe and familiar. We resisted the temptations laid before us to come back, join the fold, and be the same.

The reasons we had left and didn't want to return to our old routines revealed themselves to us in an ongoing process. One day I came across this. In the May 25, 1947, issue of *The New York Times Sunday Magazine,* Simone de Beauvoir made the following observation about Americans:

> In the United States one is always concerned to find out what an individual does and not what he [she] is; one takes it for granted that he is nothing but what he has done or may do; his purely inner reality is regarded with indifference, if, indeed, any note is taken of it. A man [woman] to be respected is one who has done things that have value.

Do or be, that was the question. Whether 'twas nobler to rake in the bucks and have no time for anyone or anything else, or get a life, had been the question in the beginning. Now I knew the answer that was right for me. Been there, done that. Now it was time to really raise the barre and test our mettle, not our margins. The Rockettes in my head said, "What about the money, honey? How you gonna keep it down to franks and beans, once you've done Lutèce?" Although the matter of money still mattered, we had experienced a much simpler way of living on the road that we thought would translate into living well anywhere but New York.

If time was indeed money, as the old saw went, I reviewed how I had spent the first several weeks at home. What was it worth to have the time to spend a couple of days with an old friend visiting from out of town who had recently lost her mate; have Alex and Fiona come up from Austin to spend his thirtieth birthday with us; take the whole family, including my eighty-plus-year-old parents, out for a long leisurely Sunday brunch;

gather old clothes for donating to the hospital and books for the library in town; finally put all those photos in an album so you could share them with your friends; volunteer some time at an organization we both believed in; read a couple of books; have friends over for a homemade dinner, not take-out Chinese. Also, for the first time ever, I really enjoyed planning and preparing a few get-togethers for the holiday season. What was the do/be ratio here?

Coming back to the Northeast in early November, when everything looked hard cold and metallic, from the steely sky to the burnished-naked trees, made me see it as a place I could leave. Maybe not forever, but for longer periods of time than I'd once thought possible. It snowed in Vermont at Thanksgiving and would be muddy in the spring until June. Not for me anymore those twenty-below mornings when starting the car was a major event. I was tired of being on the inside looking out. I wanted out—but where to, and what was I leaving behind?

I interviewed myself constantly. Journalism 101: start with the *W* words.

Who we were was evolving. We no longer had job titles to present to strangers, and we cringed when described as "retired." We were explorers in the new territory of life I'd dubbed the third quarter. If the first quarter is for education, the second for career track and family building, and the fourth is retirement, we were third-quarter conquistadors, blazing trails into the territory between building it up and giving it away.

Where to do the evolving—that was the question. Gloomy weather, high taxes, and a big mortgage made our current setup far from ideal. On the road we had realized we needed very few things in order to be happy. Where would we keep them? New Mexico had charmed us, but there were plenty of places left to visit.

What we would do was beginning to have a shape, if not a name. We wanted to find work that was engaging and fulfilling, but we were no longer willing to accept the hallucination that working was living. It seemed logical to use our experience in publishing in some way, preferably together. If possible, I wanted to take a more smorgasbord approach to working: writing, editing, and teaching all had their appeal. (I noticed that Thomas Jefferson and Ben Franklin, for example, are constantly referred to with the honorific "Renaissance men." Why are people in our era who enjoy a multitude of things generally seen as "unfocused"?)

When was more or less now.

Revising the do/be ratio required concentration. What counted as work? Who was doing the counting? Was money the only understood measure of value? Why did it seem to matter so much more once we got home? Why was Martha Stewart respected for making perfect pies and petunia beds, yet when the rest of us did those things, the world hardly noticed or, worse, sneered at our simplemindedness? Our friends and family politely asked us what our plans were. Inside it felt more like subways coming at us from all directions, trying to sweep us off our feet this way and that. Finding our way through the maze of expectations, unverbalized desires, and the need for security was a lot tougher than reading road maps to and from Alaska.

On the road we never questioned the value of our day, the worthiness of how we were living, or judged ourselves in the light of how our time was spent. What was measured was the amount of happiness, the lack of anxiety, and the quality of sleep. At home, as much as I tried to hang on to these feelings, I began to feel them slip away. I made Thanksgiving dinner and baked Christmas cookies. We hosted a cocktail party for fifty. In the city we had meetings with colleagues and dinners with friends. We pruned the yard and prepared the house for winter. We made another bid on the company in New England, but the business was sold to someone else. I wrote an article for a travel magazine while Sandy did research for a campground guide. Together we developed a plan for a series of books we might produce for a publisher. All of this took place in the first month we were home. And still we were pressed, by well-meaning friends, about what we were really going to do, as if we were not doing anything at all. Certainly it seemed, from the reactions to us, that what we were doing didn't count. Inevitably the probing led to the question of how we were going to make money. We needed to make money, and we did: I from writing, Sandy from consulting. Yet that didn't seem "real" somehow. Plain and simple: If it didn't result in a paycheck, it didn't count for much. That's why Martha Stewart's Thanksgiving was a national event while mine was just a turkey.

We had difficulty getting people to believe, and at the same time reinforcing to ourselves, that we really really really had been thoroughly and deeply happy in that $35,000, 240-square-foot motor home. Living in it might not be the exact way we wanted to spend the rest of our lives (maybe it was?), but it made crystal clear the fact that the alternative—working crazy hours to support a house we had very little time to be in—wasn't the design for the future. He who dies with the most toys is still dead, no? Who was rationalizing and who was in denial? Were we trying to make the best of a new situation? Was there a degree of jealousy in the people we talked to? Finally, at what point and how do you disengage from "society" or at least get rewired? This was our new quest: to be able to be in the world of business but not of it. To continue to be mentally stimulated by ideas and have a so-called life of the mind, but not to sell our souls to do it. Thus began our search for a new middle ground, some previously unknown emotional region where life would be engaging enough yet at the same time would not require a constant flow of adrenaline. I wanted very much to reduce my own dependence on outside stimulation, and by extension its evaluation.

How do you know how you're doing when the report cards stop coming? How were we to measure plans for our new life if not in dollars and cents? We're a nation of reportniks. All through school we are graded; then, once we're in the "real" world, annual reviews serve much the same purpose: to tell us how we're doing compared with our peers and according to the rules of the organization. Over the years I had come to accept these positive reviews as a sign of achievement. I had done well, I received raises. Some years I even made out extremely well in the bonus pool. My last year's bonus had been my best ever, yet by that point I had mentally checked out. I knew I was no longer giving my best performance, and yet the report card told me otherwise. Perhaps it was simply a case of jet lag: I was living off an earlier hot streak. Or perhaps the evaluations meant nothing at all and the money was a tasty but untrustworthy measurement. Could I live life in a pass/fail system, or would it be too bland?

*   *   *

Hunting and pecking our way around the unmapped world of refashioning a life, we continued to be haunted by images of Santa Fe. Needing a reality check, we returned (by plane) for five days in January. We made business appointments and social plans, attended theater, and roamed the galleries. On Sandy's birthday we soaked in an outdoor hot tub for two as the ice froze on the deck around us, then had full-body massages. It was always sunny, and the food was as good as we remembered, the art even better. Opportunities and connections seemed to materialize. Comforts and possibilities were everywhere. Energized and emboldened, we returned east, home for now, to continue making the necessary arrangements and rearrangements for a life.

We had changed. We had distinctly new relationships with time and money, for instance. The diet of taking time in larger portions, not broken up into little bitty bites, that we'd first become aware of back in Canada, was tremendously satisfying and successful. I had always watched my watch as I tried to get from one meeting to the next, one part of town to the other. I'd sweat it out while the taxi meter ticked away. I'd never felt I had enough time. Somehow I was more in sync now, not fighting the clock. When I had a stream of appointments in the city, I'd leave the house on time, then walk or take public transportation to my destination. I always seemed to arrive early. Instead of chopping up the interim time into watched minutes as they ticked away, I'd read the paper or relax. I saved time, money, and aggravation.

Money still mattered, but almost unconsciously we made do with less. One day I agreed to answer a telephone survey. After questions about my age, my education level, and our previous year's household income, I was asked whether I'd purchased a pair of shoes for fifty dollars or more in the previous year. I thought about it and realized I hadn't. The surveyor was stunned. She had to end the interview. I no longer fit my own profile, apparently. Sandy and I enjoyed, and had the time, to entertain our friends at home. New Yorkers love having someone make lunch or dinner for them. It's considered a novelty. Coincidentally, it costs less. Our clothing expenses all but disappeared. (While cleaning out my drawers, I unearthed a lifetime supply of pantyhose, among other things.) We discovered the deliciously illicit sensation of going to midweek bargain movie matinees and buying half-price tickets to Broadway shows. The need for recreational shopping, as an antidote to stress, was gone. Since we didn't know where we'd be living, buying things for the house seemed foolish.

There were still many questions—the final results were not in. We knew with certainty, however, that we were happy, lucky, and grateful to be where we were. Wherever that was. If life was not yet neatly tied up in a ribbon, we understood that enjoying the process of living is worthwhile.

I kept remembering a Spanish proverb I'd always liked.

LIVING WELL IS THE BEST REVENGE.

And it has nothing to do with money.

26

The Beginning

The winter following our trip was the snowiest on record in the Northeast. Our steep driveway was graced with a hundred inches or so. Susie looked good in white. Sandy says he's glad he married a woman with "the shoveling gene," since every time a few flakes fell, I was happy to be out there moving the mess. It was about the only thing that got me out of the house. I spent the winter, between shoveling episodes, writing this book. Shoveling of a different sort, some might say, but be kind.

When you're a book editor, people always ask whether you want to write. In fact, aside from a few newspaper articles, it had never occurred to me, until an editor friend encouraged me to think about it before we left. I kept our conversation to myself until I produced a draft. For the first time since leaving my job eight months earlier, I held a manuscript in my hands. It was mine, and it felt great. Together with my editor, I worked on polishing it, putting on the finishing touches. It was odd to be the recipient of her instructions, to be on the other side of the desk, but it suited my newly articulated desire to apply myself in a variety of directions.

For all those years Sandy and I had both worn our blinders firmly in place and were excellent workhorses. We believed in one way of working and accepted the way of life that it produced. Now we were moving around more freely, spending more time with those we cared about, and opening our minds to new ideas about work, even if that meant having fewer material compensations. One thing writing taught me is that I still love to work, to produce results, to achieve goals. One thing I learned about writing is that sometimes only a cliché will do—that's how they got to be clichés. Time is money. We want to grow rich together in years of satisfaction, hours of fulfillment, and minutes of pleasure.

Through this cold winter, while I wrote the book, Sandy gathered information, wrote letters, and made contact with people in Santa Fe, the place that continued to capture our imagination. We often reminded each other how bright the sun and sky were there. When we went for those exploratory meetings in January, it was cold, but the light was just as we'd remembered it. Since we returned, some of those connections have yielded concrete results, others haven't. We went through a spell of severe disappointment. We recognized that we might have to begin from scratch, whatever venture we settled on, rather than team up with someone already in business. We also heard about opportunities in areas that interested us that we'd never considered before as businesses: food, gardening, and seminars. Starting a new business is more difficult than partnering with others who already have some sort of infrastructure. It would take longer to get up and running, but in the end, hopefully, we would have what we thought we wanted: something of our own.

The process of learning to live with fluctuation, with uncertainty and unpredictability, was vexing for us. At the same time we knew it was at the core of what we were trying to achieve: We were going to learn to be flexible, even if it killed us. Ultimately, as studious as we were about laying various foundations for projects we might undertake, we couldn't separate the doing from the being any longer. We could test the waters long distance only for so long—soon we were going to have to jump in. If Santa Fe turned out not to be "it," we'd pack up the Sue and keep driving.

* * *

Eventually the scales of time tipped in our favor—daylight returned, and the snow finally melted. We began to do the mother of all spring cleanings to get the house in shape to put on the market. Before the trip I could never have imagined selling it. Then I saw the possibility of living elsewhere and admitted it might be possible to leave our homey old house. I recanted somewhat after spending the winter tucked cozily under its eaves, gazing at the two-story stone fireplace on the one hand and the frozen lake on the other while I wrote. I felt reattached to this nest. Then one afternoon as I worked, the cats dozed, and Sandy was out, I heard a tremendous "boom." My first thought was that the roof had given way from the weight of all the snow and ice. Pete and Norm looked up from their naps at me, annoyed and startled, as if to say "Okay, you're the human, you check it out." By the time I was mobile, I heard water gushing from the upstairs bathroom into our newly renovated kitchen below. I recruited every pot, pan, and bowl I could find as our carefully handpainted floor disappeared beneath inches of water. I bailed as fast as I could. The cats came by to see what great new game I was playing but doubled back hastily when they saw the wet chaos. I dialed Sandy. No answer. I dialed a friend and got his machine. I was about to dial another when the phone went dead. For all I knew about how houses worked, this was the last thing that happened before it would incinerate itself. Just then Sandy came home, took one look at the cascading water, made a U-turn, and ran to the basement. In minutes the flood stopped. So did my undying love for the house. That was it. I wanted a divorce.

Over and over again we contemplated and discussed being separated from our friends. My father made dire predictions that long-distance relationships would flicker and die. On the contrary, we decided, friends who were really friends would always be with us, no matter where we were. We kept up the habit of e-mailing new and old friends: Gladys and Lyman spent six weeks this spring flightseeing "outside," Betty's been on QVC three times, and John and Joel are visiting us from Santa Fe this summer. "Networking," we know, can be attended to electronically and on the regular visits we plan to make back to New York City. One evening we had a long conversation with my parents, explaining to them the reasons we wanted to spend time in another part of the country working for ourselves. I know it wasn't easy for these octogenarians to understand, but they stood by us and wished us godspeed. We promised to spend the summer with them in the East.

I ask everyone I meet whether they have any advice for us, if they know anyone who's quit their job, moved to another part of the country, rewritten their lives. Mostly people volunteer stories about someone they know who's retired to Arizona or San Diego or even Santa Fe, and they give us an emotional pat on the back for trying something new. I think of what we learned from the ranger at Mount Ranier about trees, twisting themselves beneath the bark to strengthen themselves against crises. This voluntary revision in our lives is surely no crisis, but it has caused me to pull myself together, take note of where my strengths are, shore up my natural defenses, and come to grips with my weaknesses. It has also allowed me to acknowledge that some of the things I loved as a child—being outdoors, learning about the world, doing new things, having a best friend at my side when I wake up in the morning—are worth preserving and cultivating as an adult. We know we can do our jobs. Now we want to be happy and learn some new things.

*   *   *

We will leave here in the fall, before darkness sets in, drive the Sue out west and stay in it until we find a place to live. The world is vast and beautiful. I want to be in it, of it. This is the beginning.

Every journey has a secret destination of which the traveler is unaware.

—Martin Buber

Who knows?

With gratitude:
to Leslie for her inspiration
and faith
to Cherise for her patience
and skill
to Richard for his calmness
under pressure of all kinds.

MARILYN J. ABRAHAM was born and raised in Washington Heights, New York. She attended Hunter College High School and the Juilliard School for the Performing Arts, Preparatory Division, graduated from Boston University and received a master's degree from Teacher's College, Columbia University. Before quitting her job and getting on the road to a new life, Marilyn Abraham was vice president and editor in chief at Prentice-Hall and later, at Simon & Schuster trade paperbacks. She and her husband, Sandy MacGregor, now live in Santa Fe, New Mexico.